Understanding Business Ethi

Also available

Supervisory Management, Fifth Edition: Evans
Informative Writing, Second Edition: Goddard
Passing Exams: Hamilton
Twelve Steps to Study Success: Lashley and Best
How to Get into Advertising: Neidle
Effective Crisis Management: Seymour and Moore
Self-Employment: Spencer and Pruss
Operations Management, Sixth Edition: Wild

UNDERSTANDING BUSINESS ETHICS

Roger Bradburn

CONTINUUM
London and New York

Continuum
The Tower Building
11 York Road
London SE1 7NX

370 Lexington Avenue
New York
NY 10017-6503

www.continuumbooks.com

First published 2001

British Library Cataloguing-in-Publication Data
A catalogue record for this book is available from the British Library.

ISBN 0-8264-5331-7(hb)
0-8264-5332-5(pb)

Typeset by Paston PrePress Ltd, Beccles, Suffolk
Printed and bound in Great Britain by TJ International, Padstow, Cornwall

Contents

CHAPTER 1

Introducing Business Ethics

Imagine that you are the ruler of the world. You have total power over everything that happens on the planet. You are faced with the following dilemmas:

1. You can almost completely remove hunger from the face of the planet. Unfortunately, to do so will involve you killing one million people. The reason for this is not clear – you just have to and there is no way out.
2. You can reduce hunger in the world by 20 per cent from its current level. This is still clearly a desirable outcome. Again though, there is a down side. In this case, you have to kill one hundred people.
3. You can leave things as they are. There is no trade off whatsoever in this case.

What do you do? There are a number of other rules that you should note:

1. Whichever decision you make, you will not kill yourself.
2. The people you kill if you adopt options 1 or 2 will all be complete strangers to you. You will not be killing friends or relatives.

This is clearly a difficult decision. If you take option 1, then you will be achieving something that mankind has failed to achieve in all its years of existence. On the other hand, killing a large number of people like that is a frightening prospect. Option 2 is still very desirable and benefits a lot of people for a relatively small down side. After all, what are 100 people out of six billion? This one hundred people might all get run over by a bus tomorrow anyway!

Option 3 does not have the benefits of the other options. However, it does not have the drawbacks either. You might take the view that killing is just plain wrong. No matter what the benefit is, there are just some things that you should not do.

Which of these is right? Clearly, this is very much an ethical dilemma.

Pause for thought ...
Present this case to a number of your colleagues at work or fellow students. Which one do they choose and why? My guess is that a majority will go for option 2. This has the advantage of being a 'classic compromise' that benefits a lot of people with only a relatively small cost. Is this what you found?

Today, every manager is faced with ethical dilemmas in their decision-making. But how might we define ethics? If you look up the word 'ethics' in any dictionary, you will find such terms as 'morals', 'doing the right thing', and so forth. But what is 'doing the right thing'? Over the centuries, various philosophers have tried to provide us with sets of rules to assist us. In truth though, there is no perfect set of ethical rules. What this book aims to achieve is to make you aware of some of the key ethical issues that managers might face to make you think about the possible solutions. Considerable use will be made of case studies. These studies will highlight some of the most famous ethical dilemmas presented to managers over the years.

A Very New Old Subject

Business ethics is often described as a very new old subject. This might seem a rather strange statement, but it reflects the development of the discipline. On the one hand, ethical thinking has its roots in the writings of the great philosophers such as Socrates and Confucius. On the other, as an academic subject it has only really come of age since the 'Wall Street' scandals of the 1980s. This period of greed shocked many observers and started them to think about what sort of managers were being developed. Of course, most were graduates from the major business schools! As a result of this, business ethics has become an important subject throughout the world. The section at the end of this first chapter will consider the development of this subject in more depth. For now, it is important to note that business ethics is not just about being moral and doing the right thing. It is also true to say that increasingly organizations throughout the world are finding that adopting an ethical approach has many advantages from a business strategy point of view. Having an ethical policy can reduce the attention of pressure groups and often save the company huge sums of money. Acting ethically may be fundamental to the company's very existence. Throughout this book there are many cases of companies that have acted in a very unethical manner and regretted it.

In this first section, we will consider some of the philosophical views that we might apply to ethical dilemmas.

The Foundation of Ethical Decision-Making

Traditionally, there have been two broad schools of thought in modern ethics, which have developed over the years. The two main groups are teleological ethics and deontological ethics.

Teleological Ethics

In its purest sense primarily focuses on the 'ends', the results of the decision rather than the method of getting to that result. A typical teleological view might be that the 'ends justify the means'.

Deontological Ethics

In its purest sense focuses on the *means* of getting to the result. It takes the view that how you get there is as important as to where you get. In the 'ruler of the world' case above, a teleological view might be that reducing or removing hunger from the world would be a highly desirable result and that the fact that you had to kill a small number of people would be an acceptable fact. A deontological view would be more along the lines that there are certain things that you should simply not do, such as killing. Deontology considers such factors as morals, rules and justice.

Consider the difference between these two examples in the following case:

CASE STUDY – **Mr Smith and Mrs Jones**

Two sales people, Mr Smith and Mrs Jones are both trying to win a desirable order for their business. Both are in the same situation in that their companies are struggling and to lose the business would almost certainly result in mass redundancies. It is also very likely that the losing sales person will lose their job as well.

Mr Smith takes the teleological approach. He reasons that he has to get the order because if he doesn't then he would lose the business.

Losing the business would have a very adverse effect on the lives of many people in his company. In addition there would be the lost business for the company's suppliers and so forth. He might therefore reason that anything that he does to get the order is acceptable because the ends justify the means. What 'anything' means clearly has its limits for everyone. However, he might consider that bribery or sabotaging the competition might be acceptable under certain conditions.

Mrs Jones takes a deontological approach. She would take the view that getting the order is clearly an important factor, but not at any cost. She has certain rules – morals if you like – that she would stick to, irrespective of the outcome. She might take the view that bribery can never be justified, for example.

Having introduced the basic idea, we should now look at these two main schools of thought in some detail.

Teleological Ethics

There are a number of different forms of teleological ethics that have been developed over the years. These include ethical egoism, utilitarianism and Machiavellianism. We shall now consider each of these in turn.

Ethical Egoism

'All people are selfish at heart.' Many people, when confronted with the question of what motivates an individual's morality will make this assertion. Ethical egoism supports this view and suggests that a person should act in a way that maximizes his or her own long-term interests. Writers such as Hobbes suggested that ultimately we are all genetically programmed to do what is right for us. We might show an interest in others, but if we do, it is only because it is in our own self-interest to do so.

If we accept this, then we would have to take the view that morality really means nothing. It would also suggest that we always put our own interest first. It would also tend to put a very large question mark over the whole concept of business ethics. Surely, everyone in business is just looking to pursue his or her own interests, so why would anyone be ethical?

There are some basic problems with this rather cynical view. The idea that everyone is selfish and does not care about others would not seem to be supported by reality. There have been many cases of selfless acts through the ages, of people helping others to the detriment of their own aims. Of course, it could easily be argued by a cynic that these people who did selfless deeds were pursuing their own aims. They were looking to make themselves famous by doing these acts.

This type of argument would seem to fall down if you consider reality. Many people who committed selfless acts – such as the people of the French Resistance during the Second World War who helped allied airmen escape – had no real hope or thought of becoming famous. There was clearly more to it than that.

Pause for thought ...
When was the last time you did something that genuinely put the other person first? Why did you do it? What were your motivations? Do people commit selfless acts in business? Why do you feel that way?

There is another aspect of egoism, which should be considered. Is egoism really selfish anyway? Supporters of an ethical egoist approach might argue that if everybody looked after his or her own *genuine* best interests, society as a whole would benefit. An example might be the case of litter. Littering is ultimately of no benefit to anybody, it could be argued, so if everybody follows their own best interest, they would not litter. You might find this a difficult idea to accept. Clearly there will be cases where looking after your own interests, no matter how genuine, would not be acceptable. Sometimes you have to put others first. Later in this chapter, we will look at the idea of NORM and enlightened egoism to consider how egoism might be used in modern management.

Utilitarianism

This view puts forward the idea that a person should act in a way that maximizes the good of the greatest number of people. A good example of this was seen in the 'ruler of the world' case. Clearly on the face of it, choosing one of the first two options would seem to be the best when it comes to maximizing the greatest number of people. There are problems with this though, as we have seen.

The eighteenth-century philosopher Jeremy Bentham originally put the idea of utilitarianism forward, although the main promoter of it was the nineteenth-century philosopher John Stuart Mill. Mill believed that our aim should always be the greatest happiness for the greatest number. To him, there was a simple logic in all of this. As everybody desires happiness then logically happiness has to be a correct aim.

Mill was what is known as a hedonist. This is someone who believes that you should always maximize pleasure. Clearly there are limitations to this. Indeed, later-utilitarian writers have argued that pleasure is too wide and vague an idea and that we should maximize other things such as friendship or knowledge or morals.

How might we put this into practice? Utilitarians have put forward a number of basic rules that we should use in making teleological decision-making. These are as follows:

1. Under utilitarianism everybody is deemed equal, irrespective of race, religion, intelligence or any other personal characteristic.
2. You do have to take into account the long-term consequences – whose pleasure? For example, in the short term we might achieve more happiness by polluting the planet (many environmentalists would argue that that is indeed what we are doing), but what about those people coming along in future generations?
3. Pleasure is measured in total. This means that the great unhappiness of one person might outweigh the pleasure experienced by lots of other people. In the 'rule of the world' case, this might go against our view that we should kill a few people to the benefit of the majority. Those people who have been killed have certainly experienced a lot of unhappiness! On the other hand, how do you measure happiness? Can the great unhappiness of 100 people outweigh the considerable happiness of millions, many of whom would have died from starvation if we had not taken the decision! This is one of the great problems of utilitarianism.
4. What is pleasure anyway? Utilitarians also argue that some pleasures are *qualitatively* better than others are. We might take the view that intellectual pleasure is a more desirable pleasure than most. Rather famously, John Stuart Mill once wrote that it was 'better to be Socrates unsatisfied than a pig satisfied'.

So how do you decide which is more pleasurable? Mill's solution was for you to ask all the people involved about how desirable or undesirable the result was and take a decision based on this. Clearly this is a very subjective issue – a common problem in this discipline.

Utilitarianism and the Manager

What does all of this mean in real life and business? The fact is that most managers take utilitarian decisions every day. Utilitarianism is really a form of cost-benefit analysis. A company could justify concealing from construction workers the dangers of removing asbestos from a school building because of the benefits gained by all the future schoolchildren. There are a number of legal cases with the environmental protection agency in the USA where companies have complained that the cost of compliance with pollution control may be too great given the small number of people affected. Some of the classic cases that we will discuss, such as the Ford Pinto, certainly had a form of cost-benefit analysis in their decision-making. Is this always the right approach, though?

A Critique of Utilitarianism

Utilitarianism has received much criticism. Perhaps the most serious one is that it is not possible to account for *justice*. The utilitarian believes that the aim should be the maximum pleasure or outcome for the majority. On this basis a minority would suffer. The famous ethics writer Ronald Green once made this point. If the maximum pleasure was achieved by putting a small percentage of society in slavery then it is hard for utilitarians to argue against this following their basic rules. We can see the same basic problem in our 'ruler of the world' case. The minority who are to be killed have clearly not received a very good deal. Is killing people just?

The second problem, is what is to be maximized? Should we maximize for pleasure, happiness, friendship or whatever? As we have seen, utilitarians have never really answered this question. Another problem is this, what do we do if they conflict? Sometimes, one form of pleasure will result in a lot of displeasure. Which one do we take into account?

The fact still remains that most of us do take teleological decisions in our day-to-day lives. With much of our decision-making we simply weigh the consequences of our actions before making decisions. We make predictions. We chose a college because of the consequences of choice. We are told by numerous motivational writers that we should sit down and write out a number of goals. The things we really want. Do we really take enough time to think about the rights and wrongs of how we get there?

Machiavellianism

This is perhaps the most extreme version of teleological thinking. Essentially it involves doing what you have to do to get the job done. Another word that is often used for it is expediency. This view denies the existence of morals. Every decision has to be made on the basis of the facts presented at that point.

How practical is this view in life and business?

Undoubtedly there will be times when an expedient view is necessary such as in cases of emergency. Machiavellian decisions are undoubtedly taken all the time in war and no doubt in the boardroom. However, a society without morals would clearly have its limitations. No rules would equal chaos and anarchy. One problem that managers do face, and which is well illustrated in some of the cases in this text, is that it is often very difficult to know where to draw the line. The business world is very tough these days and we are all under pressure. Often we have to take tough decisions that we might not really want to take. There is a very real danger that we push the line of acceptability too far. It is so easy to convince ourselves that 'it's OK, really' and move on, even when we should really have stopped and thought. There are a number of cases in this book where people have undoubtedly been killed as a result of managers taking expedient decisions without thinking about the morality of the decision or the long-term consequences.

Deontological Theories

The word 'deontology' comes from the Greek word for duty and this type of thinking represents a very different approach to the teleological and utilitarian approaches discussed above. Deontologists believe that what is crucial are the rules and principles that guide reasoning. Essentially the means are just as important as the ends. Over the years a variety of writers have put forward a number of variations of this view. Perhaps the best known is that put forward by Immanuel Kant.

Kant's main view is that all things in this world may have value but they may be detrimental too. Thus wealth, beauty and intelligence may be beneficial but they can be bad if they are used selfishly. Even happiness can create complacency. On this basis the utilitarian view that says maximizing pleasure is desirable is unsound. There will be times when pleasure is simply not right, even though it is desired by many. For example, we might all desire to drive around in high-performance, 'gas-guzzling' cars. These cars certainly give a lot of pleasure. However, they also pollute the atmosphere and use a large mount of oil. Oil can be used for many other purposes, such as producing plastics and other products. It can be argued that just burning it is really rather wasteful and that driving high-performance cars is therefore not acceptable, even though the majority of us would certainly like to!

Kant's key belief was that you should do things according to your duty. But what is your duty? Kant explained the idea of duty in the following way. First, one ought only to act such that the principles of one's act could become a universal law of human action in a world in which one would hope to live. This is rather like the view put forward in many religions. 'Do unto others as you would like done unto you' is a view put forward by Christianity and other religions and is a common moral view.

Consider another question. Is it acceptable to lie? You might say that really it is not, but most people lie at some point in their lives. Taking Kant's ideas, what would happen if we all lied all of the time?

Well, the world would be in total chaos, I would suggest. How could we trust anyone? By definition, we could not. We would turn the TV on to watch an advert that was full of lies and then a news programme that was also completely flawed. Only we would not be able to turn the set on because the guy who installed it had lied about it being a working model!

If we do an act or make a statement, Kant would suggest that we would need to ask ourselves would this be acceptable as a universal rule? Can we always work to universal rules, though? Are there exceptions in life? I would suggest that there are and that for this reason Kant's deontology may have its limitations.

Kant's second point was that you should respect everybody as a rational and free being. In other words, all of your decision-making should be made on the basis of respect. The great motivational writer, Earl Nightingale, once put forward the view that you should treat everyone that you meet as if they are the most important person in the whole world. The reason for this is that, as far as they are concerned, they are!

There have been other deontological views put forward over the years. Two good examples are the ideas of Locke and Rawls.

Locke argued that everybody is born with certain natural rights – they cannot be taken away and this should therefore be a fundamental grounding of any ethical decision. Whatever the decision, there will be certain human rights, such as freedom of speech, which will have to be taken into account before any decision is made.

John Rawls put forward the idea of 'the veil of ignorance'. He asks, what would you do if you were under a veil of ignorance? If you did not know who you were, rich or poor, male or female, motivated or lazy, which principles would you choose? The point of this is clear. We should really take decisions based on an altruistic view that is not influenced by who we are, who we know and what our motivations are. Essentially, every decision should be based on a level playing field. How many times are your principles dictated by *who* you are?

Whichever view we take, deontology can be summarized around the following key issues:

1. There should be rules and morals in society that should be fair to everyone and that should universally apply.
2. These rules should hold universally even over the passage of time. A decision made today should not have a predictable adverse comment in the future.
3. All members of society under deontology should be treated with equal respect.

Pause for thought ...
How often do you make decisions based on deontological thinking? How important are rules and morals in life? What might be a limitation of this view – always working to rules? Are there ever exceptions in your work or life? How might you cope with these?

Perhaps the biggest problem with deontological thinking is that it does not take into account exceptions. Things which fall outside the normal set of rules. We shall therefore consider some other approaches that have been put forward.

Ronald Green and NORM

The work of Ronald Green is well known in the business ethics sphere and his views have provided considerable insight for the manager. NORM is short for:

Neutral
Omnipartial
Rule
Making

The approach essentially tries to combine the best aspects of the main teleological and deontological approaches already discussed. NORM suggests that on the one hand, there has to be a procedure of choice. We have to have some rules that assist us in deciding which way we go. This might be a view that we benefit the majority, for example. On the other hand, NORM also recognizes the importance of morality, fairness and common sense. Green argues that the question of what is acceptable is not a question of what the majority want, but as a result of the free consensus of all people in society. Taking our high-performance car example, the majority might want these cars, but the free consensus of society is that we should not really pollute the planet. There is a 'you are right, really' aspect to this thinking. Green's view also takes into account the minorities of society on any decision in a way that utilitarianism cannot. He also goes on to point out that setting universal rules has its limitations as well. The fact is that we all have our own views and make our own decisions. As a result of this there are few acts that have been universally condemned. Even evil actions have been supported by some. At the time of writing, there are many that would support the actions of Adolph Hitler and the Third Reich along with the Holocaust. We might well regard them as extremists, but they certainly exist. In simple terms then, it is difficult to produce a set of universal rules that we can always apply in the way that Kant would suggest. So what can we do? Green's answer is the idea of omnipartiality. This asks us to take into account the beliefs and feelings of all concerned – the stakeholders in the decision – and take an impartial, neutral decision. It is what we often call even-handedness. Green sees the modern manager as a rational individual who has to balance competing claims and make normative decisions.

Perhaps we might conclude from this that there are many approaches to morality that the manager might adopt. Knowing which one to adopt can be a very difficult decision because all of the views have their own merits. An interesting compromise view is that taken by James Rachels. Rachels suggests that irrespective of all of these differing views, in the end there are two main criteria that we need in order to achieve a minimum conception of morality. These are *reason* and *impartiality*. Let us consider what he means by these terms. In the case of reason Rachels means that a moral decision must be based on reasons acceptable to other rational persons. This is rather like the view of Kant and his 'universal rule'. In other words, if a decision taken were the sort of decision that most rational people would take then it looks as though it will be acceptable and a moral thing to do. The criterion of impartiality is achieved when the interests of all those affected by a moral decision are taken into account. This follows the ideas of Green's NORM to a point.

We could thus say that a decision is morally correct when the decision proves to be rational and impartial. It is really a cross between teleological and deontological decision-making.

Values

So far we have spoken about decision-making. However, this is only part of the moral process. A very important aspect is the area of values.

All individuals and organizations have codes of ethics based on their values. Values are the core beliefs or desires that guide or motivate attitudes and actions. We have already seen how ethics is concerned with how a person should behave. What is right and what is wrong? Values are more concerned with explaining why a person behaves the way they do, 'this is what I believe in', but the fact that this underpins the thought process of managers makes it a worthwhile topic to consider.

Values are learnt early in life. They come from a variety of sources including our parents, our friends and our school. An important contributing factor is the culture that we are born into and a very important question that we will consider is this. Cultures have different ways of dealing with problems. Inevitably, therefore, ethics will vary according to the culture of the person. Does this mean that there is no such thing as a universal set of ethics? This question revolves around an idea known as 'ethical relivatism'. This suggests that an ethical decision is right providing it matches the cultural values in the country in which the decision was taken. Thus bribery might not be right in some countries but it is certainly right in others. We will discuss the concept of ethical relivatism shortly.

The Influence of Values on Decision-Making

As adults we often seek environments that are compatible with the values that we learnt as children. They may also influence motivation and decision-making later on in life. There is much evidence that people who have the same values as the organization in which they work are much more likely to be motivated by those values as well. We often hear talk of a person's 'face fitting' in an organization – or not, as the case may be.

Are there some values that are more important than others? The ethics writer Rokeach suggested that there are two main types of values. These are:

1. *Terminal values* – These are desirable end states or goals, something that we are trying to achieve. Terminal values can be further split into two, namely *personal values* which might include the things that we want out of life – a happy home, children, good health or whatever it is – and *social values* which cover things in life generally. These might encompass such things as peace on earth, the end of poverty, a cure for cancer or whatever.
2. *Instrumental values* – These relate to preferable modes of behaviour or the means of achieving one's terminal values. There are again two types of instrumental values. The first of these clearly relates into ethical decision-making and are our moral values. These might include honesty, being reliable or whatever. Moral values are important to us and we normally feel guilty or unhappy if we are forced to break a moral value. As a result of this, our ethical decision-making may well be influenced by our moral values. The second area of values in the instrumental area is competence values. These are values that we aspire to in terms of personal performance. These might include being ambitious, competent at our job, being attractive to the opposite sex, or having high intellectual capability. These things are important to us. They are what matters to us and if we fail to meet these goals we feel inadequate, etc. Naturally, we may want to avoid such a situation and our ethical decision-making may well reflect this.

Ethical Versus Non-Ethical Values

Not all values have an ethical component. Some values are clearly ethical in that they relate to right and wrong. There are a number of underlying ethical values that you would find in most parts of the US and similar cultures. These might include:

- honesty;
- respect;
- being reliable;
- being fair;
- caring for others;
- doing the right thing and being an honest citizen.

> Pause for thought ... What would you regard as being the values of the society that you live in? How do these compare with the organization that you work in?

Non-ethical values deal with things such as things that we like or desire. Examples might include money, fame, status, happiness, personal freedom, etc. Generally we would suggest that in the order of things, ethical decision-making would be ahead of non-ethical. We should put ethics before fame perhaps. However, how many examples can you think of where the non-ethical value took precedent?

Moral Reasoning

This is another key area in the decision-making process. Essentially we are talking about the way that we think things through. The fact is that values alone do not determine our actions. Our behaviour is also controlled by moral reasoning, organizational and national culture, the influence of significant people in our lives, past and present and whether or not our decision is going to harm others or ourselves.

Is all moral reasoning the same? Most writers would say that there are three types of moral reasoning. We should now briefly consider these now.

The lowest level of moral reasoning is known as the self-centred level. This type of reasoning has its emphasis on the consequences rather than the principle of it. In this sense it is rather teleological – if rather rudimentary. This type of reasoning is most usually found in young children who tend to see moral issues in terms of everything being black and white, right and wrong. In this type of moral reasoning their consequences rather than any other criteria judge all actions. The question will be, what is the reward of me doing this and what punishment might I suffer if I get caught? If the benefits of the result outweigh the chances of the punishment then I should do the action. It is interesting to note that as well as children, criminals often exhibit this type of reasoning. They judge actions in terms of whether or not they will get caught rather than whether or not it was a good thing to do in the first place. Morality and laws are simply not considered.

The second level of moral reasoning is known as the conformity level. The conformity level is a little more sophisticated than the self-centred form. Perhaps the main characteristic is that this type of reasoning is group related. People who think this way are primarily concerned about being loyal to the social order. It is important to do the right thing, to do what most people do. This type of moral reasoning is perhaps understandable given the social nature of humanity. People tend to read mass-market newspapers and watch popular soap operas on the TV. These provide the individual with guidelines as to what is normal and right. The emphasis is more on doing your duty rather than doing what might be really right. Interestingly enough, many motivational writers have challenged this form of moral reasoning. Coming back to Earl Nightingale, he suggested that the whole of society was rather like a convoy in times of war. The ships all bunch together and go at the speed of the slowest so as not to leave anyone behind. Nightingale also points out the folly of this and how some people break out of this and leave the majority standing. This type of thinking fits in well with the last level of moral reasoning that we will consider.

The principled level of moral reasoning recognizes the rule of law but also respects decisions of conscience. Factors like human rights and social justice are critical in this respect. Clearly people who reason at this level are not anarchists and will certainly follow most laws. However, they will tend to question decisions and views. Just because the majority thinks something is right and the government says so, they will still think about the implications and take decisions and form views based on well-researched information.

Most people's moral reasoning tends to be dominated by one stage although they may change occasionally. Education can certainly help in this respect. Most adults in Western urban society tend to be at the conformity stage. As we have seen, many prison inmates never get past the self-centred stage. The principled stage is really restricted to the better educated although there have been many exceptions to this. There is some evidence that people tend to go through the stages in order, although development is not always governed by age. Some young people reason at higher stages than their elders do. However, cognitive development – the ability to think things through – tends to develop during adolescence.

Whichever stage we are at, there can be no doubt that much of our ethical decision-making is going to be influenced by our core values and moral reasoning. Next time you make a decision – and we all make many every day – consider how much your values and moral reasoning have influenced the way you have made your decision. In view of this, was it the right decision?

CASE STUDY – ***Twelve Angry Men***

Twelve Angry Men, directed by Sidney Lumet, was produced in 1957 and is regarded by most critics as a classic. The film is about a jury of twelve men who have to decide the fate of a young Latino accused of murdering his father with a switchblade knife. The film is particularly relevant to the discussion of business ethics because it illustrates well the idea of morality. The film starts with the jury filing out of the courtroom. Very quickly, the jury takes a vote and the result is eleven to one in favour of guilty. One man votes against. This man, played by Henry Fonda, uses a rational approach to his reasoning unlike the others who are clearly making decisions based on their emotions. Several of the jurors are making decisions based on racial prejudice, the individual's appearance and other irrational criteria. During the remainder of the film, which takes place only in the jury room, Fonda turns the vote to twelve to zero for acquittal. The key point of the film is that the twelve 'angry men' all start making decisions emotionally – with the exception of Fonda – but end up all using rational approaches towards the end and make the correct decision, based on evidence rather than emotion.

Virtue Ethics

Before we move on to some specific cases in business ethics, I would like to consider one more branch of ethical thinking. All of the arguments that we have considered so far have been act based. That is to say that a person's morality and decision-making have been judged on their actions. A person has made the right ethical decision because they did the 'right thing'. As we have seen, what the 'right thing' is is a matter of opinion. It might be producing the right result or doing something that would be generally acceptable to most people. It is interesting to note, however, that the early pre-Christian philosophers took a different approach and it is worthwhile considering this for a short while.

The early Greek philosophers in particular took what is known as an 'agent-cantered' approach. These writers included such luminaries as Socrates (469–399 BC), Plato (427–347 BC) and Aristotle (384–322 BC). By 'agent cantered' we mean that the judgement of ethics and morality is based on the person rather than the act. These early thinkers believed that the important thing were the character traits of a good person. What traits were these? Well, they included courage, honesty, wisdom, temperance and generosity. Who could argue with those? Of course the main thing from our point of view is this. These early philosophers believed that what people did was important, but if you were a good person you would do the right thing anyway. Therefore the important thing was to be a good person.

It should be said that different philosophers have different views about this 'being a good person'. Aristotle believed that all people were inherently good, but sometimes they 'fell by the wayside'. He took the view that people all have inherent 'potentialities' and thus human development is basically a struggle for self-actualization. Aristotle used the example of an acorn. An acorn's aim in life is to become an oak tree, not any other form of tree, but an oak tree. If it is stunted or diseased then it is simply deficient. Aristotle took the view that all human beings are basically good. Any form of evil is a deficiency. What is more, human beings are social animals so fulfilment includes making oneself a good member of the community. All decision-making should thus be made based on the idea that all people are fundamentally good, even though they have 'fallen by the wayside' in some cases.

Whether people are inherently good is a matter of opinion. Sigmund Freud claimed we are all naturally aggressive and selfish! This is more in keeping with the egoist view previously discussed.

What can the early philosophers tell us about business ethics? Well, I think that we can all agree that the desirable character traits would indeed be very desirable in business, at least on the face of it. However, you could also argue that sometimes being honest is not always the best policy and that sometimes generosity is not the right trait to display.

The Development of Business Ethics

The remainder of this book will go on to examine ethical decision-making in a variety of business situations. However, just to complete the introduction, it would be good just to consider how this 'very new old' subject has developed over the years.

As we have seen in the first part of this chapter, ethics as a subject goes back a long time. However, in this book, the main focus is on *applied* ethics – applying ethical rules to business situations and cases. Business ethics as an applied subject really goes back to a number of scandals experienced in New York's Wall Street in 1986. Insider trading in particular shocked many people, because those involved were senior members of society and, as we have already mentioned, many of these people were business-school graduates! It had been assumed that they had learnt right and wrong not only through their education but also from their families' background and so forth. Clearly something was wrong and it needed addressing. In addition to the Wall Street scandals we can also note a range of other factors that have influenced the development of business ethics as a subject.

The Consumer Movement

The consumer movement in the USA is also a key background to business ethics. President Kennedy in 1962 declared that consumers had three rights. These are the right to safety, the right to be informed, and the right to be heard. This declaration led to the beginning of the consumer movement around 1964. The main aim of the consumer movement was to change the imbalance that had occurred between consumer and supplier after the Second World War. The period after 1945 had seen a tremendous boom in consumer purchasing. Generally speaking, demand for consumer goods had greatly outstripped the supply and the supplier had the upper hand. Poor quality and unreliability became common and it is only in more recent times that the consumer has become king. We will discuss the ethics of consumerism later on in the book and relate the ideas of this to the idea of 'total quality management'.

Ethics and the Corporate Environment

Corporate ethics is a major growth area and many companies have developed codes of ethics that set the tone of decision-making throughout the organization. Many companies have ethical codes, which fit into their overall strategy and relate to their mission statement.

Why should a company have ethical goals? In reality, there are a variety of reasons why this might be the case. In particular, we can note the following:

1. *The view of the founder* – There are many cases of organizations taking an ethical stance because of the moral values of the person or people who founded them. Examples might include The Body Shop, Levi Strauss and Co., Ben and Jerry's Ice Cream and the UK-based sandwich bar chain Pret A Manger. There is much dispute whether or not their ethical leaders are actually taking an ethical stance or simply adopting an ethical strategy because of

the business value of this approach. Either way, there can be no doubt of the importance of the founder in these cases.

2. *It is good business* – There is no question that adopting an ethical strategy is not just about being morally correct, it is also about being more successful. Reasons for adopting an ethical strategy might include:
   - Reduce the demand for consumerism. Aggressive consumer activity can sap the strength of a company and seriously tarnish the image of the organization. We might think of such examples as McDonald's and the famous 'McLibel' case and the adverse publicity experienced by Nike from their use of low-cost labour in the Far East.
   - Participating in the consumerism movement by initiating an active consumer-education programme. Working with the consumer rather than against them.
   - Cooperating with government agencies, non-profit organizations and consumer groups.

A further development is industry-wide codes of ethics. Self-regulation wards off the need for legal action by the government, for example. We shall discuss the thought processes behind codes of ethics a little later in the book.

The Societal Marketing Concept

A further way of looking at business ethics was put forward by the famous marketer Philip Kotler. He questioned whether or not the conventional marketing concept was a valid one. Marketing is about serving consumer need and the companies that do it best get the business. But this ignores the fact that by serving our customer we may well be damaging the environment or even them! Kotler pointed out the companies who produce products that create large and unnecessary amounts of litter or unhealthy fast food may well be meeting the needs of the consumer – which is really what marketing is about – but may well not be acting in a responsible way. He argued that today a company needs to be customer oriented in a responsible way. Not just give them what they want, but give them what they want and what is good for them.

Conclusion

This chapter has reviewed a range of ideas about ethics, morality and ethical decision-making. Reading through this, you might well consider that there is no easy solution to deciding what is right and what is wrong. You would be right. However, we can argue that today's manager should at least make informed decisions based on rational thought processes that take into account the views of all stakeholders involved. In business there has to be rules, as in all walks of life. However, are the rules of business the same as the rules in life generally? The next section of the book will look at this important question.

CHAPTER 2

Whose Rules Do We Play To, Anyway?

The question that I want to consider here is this: does business have a separate set of rules to life in general? In particular, should you always tell the truth? I am sure that most people would agree that they should not lie to their grandmother. But if you are faced with an angry customer and have to tell them something, what happens then? Are their certain aspects of business that makes lying acceptable? Are the rules for business more lenient (or just different) than those in other areas? We will talk about advertising later on in the text and clearly the opportunity to falsify information here is strong. But not telling the truth can cover a much wider area such as reporting compliance to government legislation or simply falsifying expense accounts.

Some would argue that business is a game of poker and that as in poker bluffing is acceptable. A very significant article is that by Albert Carr who argues that business is like poker and that as in poker some bluffing in business is essential.

The fact is that most business executives are pressured to deceive in some way in order to survive. Can we split the world into different areas of morality, though? The famous sociologist Max Weber suggested that life could be split into three moral areas. These are:

1. The private lives of everyone including family and friends, and including your grandmother, taking the example above.

2. The economic life and the market, which would certainly include business and much of what we are discussing here.
3. Politics and the affairs of state.

It can certainly be argued that modern life is much more split up than in the past. In the Middle Ages, for example, there was the state, the church, and the people. These were very much entwined. Business was also very much related to these areas. The industrial revolution and the development of modern society have really broken these ties up. Weber also points out that areas of human living such as business are really specific functional areas within society, which have very specific sets of rules. We might also add to business functions such as medicine and technology.

How reasonable is this view – a view that different parts of society should have different sets of rules? There are several views on this, which we should consider.

Views of Morality

The Unitarian View of Morality

The unitarian view argues against the Weberian view of separate moral groups. Many religions take this view, as does Marxism. A unitarian view would suggest that morals are the same irrespective of the case. Thus, lying is always wrong, irrespective of the situation in which that lying took place. You cannot simply take the view that business is business and a different set of rules applies. Modern writers in this area such as Jeurissen (1995) suggest that it is simply not practical for business to follow moral principles alone. Some things are clearly dictated by other things such as economics and market forces.

The Separation View of Morality

Many economists have written supporting this view, ranging from Adam Smith to Milton Friedman. We will discuss this view on several occasions throughout this book. Adam Smith famously talked about the 'invisible hand' of the market. Essentially the market will always produce the best solution for society and for this reason if an organization follows its prime objective, namely the maximization of its shareholder wealth, it will in the long run produce the best result for mankind as a whole. At its extreme the separatist view of society takes the view that the only thing that matters is maximizing profits. Thus we might take the view that using child labour is right because it serves to reduce the costs of companies and therefore increases their profits.

Separatists do not ignore the rule of law, but they do argue that the amount of intervention by the state in business should be minimized. Essentially laws should be produced that respect property and the workings of business, but not much else.

How acceptable is the separatist view? Surely if something is immoral, it is always immoral. As we have noted, many companies have adopted ethical policies and strategies. Whilst in some cases this is purely a positioning strategy – a desire to look 'right' in the eyes of the public – there is equally no question that the leaders of these organizations do have a genuine desire to be morally correct in many cases.

The Integration View of Morality

This view accepts that economics must be based on profit maximization but also argues that it is not realistic to split the business world from life in general. Writers such as Talcott Parsons have suggested that whilst economics was a separate sub-sphere the people who worked in this sub-sphere also lived in society in general. Do people completely change when they come home from work? Although the rules may be different it is clear that they fundamentally do not. For this reason it can be suggested that business and life in general do have some separation, but in the long run all must be covered by basic moral rules. Business is part of life, after all.

Is business bluffing acceptable? Coming back to the work of Carr, we might suggest that telling the odd untruth or bending the rules a little is acceptable, and part of the business world. I would argue that this can be very dangerous indeed. The dangers can best be illustrated by looking at a number of case studies. Read through them and then consider how acceptable you think they are:

- A young executive finds it hard to get a job because he does not have a university degree. One day, he meets someone in a bar who has recently been to a major university. He speaks to the graduate for some time and learns a great deal about the course and the university. After this, he resolves that he will put on his résumé that he also went to this university and took this course. After all, he now knows enough to sound convincing and lots of employers don't bother to check. It must have been a good idea because he got a highly paid job.
- A company president finds that an ageing executive, within a few years of retirement and his pension, is not as productive as formerly. The company is struggling a little and the ageing executive's pay cheque is causing major problems. What should the president do? Should the executive be kept on?

- An Internet-based retailer sells hunting knives through mail order. He knows very well that many of his customers are not collectors at all but use them for violent purposes. However, there is no law against selling such knives and he has no written proof that the knives are being used for this purpose, so why worry?
- The manager of a car dealership finds out that a car he bought was not quite as he imagined. The car was roadworthy but had been crashed and repaired. There was no obvious damage to the car – the repair had been done well. The manager had nothing in writing about the repair but had overheard some people in a pub telling how they had managed to sell his dealership a crash-damaged car and how they had got away with it. The manager has a potential buyer on his forecourt. Should he mention anything about this or just sell the car and let someone else worry about it?

How acceptable are these situations?

Pause for thought ... Take this list of cases and ask some of your colleagues or friends what they think Ask them two things:

1. How acceptable do you think these actions are?
2. Would they do it themselves and, above all, why?

Clearly, there are some problems with the actions in the case studies above. Some of the actions are potentially illegal, others not. You may well have found that when you asked your friends about the mini-cases they answered that it was acceptable, providing no laws were broken. After all, how much damage would lying on your résumé do providing the person could do the job?

Many people in business take the view that if you don't openly break the law and don't deliberately lie then you owe it to yourself to do everything you can to make as much money as possible. This fits in with the separatist view in that it assumes that profit maximization (subject to the laws of the land) can be the only motive in business. What if you hurt someone? Well, it might be said that if you hurt someone in the process then you should not worry about it because if you don't hurt someone then someone else will.

The Problem of 'The Line'

This view can be very dangerous. It is often said that good managers make bad ethical choices. Very often quite ordinary people make decisions, which on the face of it seem very irresponsible and totally unacceptable. A major problem is this. We may all agree that there is a point where a line has to be drawn. A point where going any further down an immoral route cannot be tolerated. The problem seems to be this. Major ethical problems in business seem to arise when a problem gets worse on an incremental basis. The 'line' is pushed a little farther and then a little farther more until a point is reached which would never have been imagined. Two cases will be used to illustrate this:

CASE STUDY 1 – **The Electronics Company**

The Electronics Company makes electronic components for the military and professional markets. It has a very good reputation and is very much the market leader in many of the market segments that it serves. Quality has been a major reason for success. The company is based in the USA and had a UK sales office, which is where this event happened. The company was very pleased to win a very large and profitable order for some of its components. These components were going to go into dosimeters, a form of Geiger counter that is used by the military to assess whether or not someone has been irradiated. Several of these dosimeters were also bound for non-military applications such as nuclear power stations. The components were produced to a high military specification and were hermetically sealed. The quality of this sealing was tested using specialized test equipment because if the seal was broken, the performance of the component could be affected and the *reading given by the dosimeter made inaccurate*. Thus someone who was irradiated could be shown as being OK and not given any treatment and someone who was perfectly OK could be told that they had been irradiated and treated accordingly. The components arrived and were immediately rejected by the customer. They were too big to fit in the dosimeters box. The correct action would have been to send the parts back to the factory, but this would take time. The company resolved to solve the problem by making the parts smaller. This was done by issuing all of their sales office employees (none of whom were trained engineers) with sharp knives and emery boards. This worked and the parts were now small enough to fit. It was then pointed out that there was now a question over the sealing. Would the parts be water-tight now that they had been modified? Really they needed to be tested but this again took time that they did not have. A quick phone call to the quality department in the USA suggested that the way to test them was to boil the parts in water and watch for air bubbles. One of the employees of the company had recently purchased a large gas oven and so it was agreed that the parts should be boiled on the hob of the oven and he and his wife (who was a professional caterer) should watch for any air bubbles. None were found so the parts were duly shipped to the military and nuclear power stations. They are still out there.

Analysis

How can we explain this behaviour? On the face of it, this was irresponsible and unprofessional, yet there was no evidence that the employees of the company were either. What is it that draws people to do things like this? Cases such as this are remarkably common and over the years there have been many classic examples. Perhaps one of the best known is that of Johns Manville.

CASE STUDY 2 – **The Manville Corporation**

For many years the Manville Corporation was regarded as being one of the strongest businesses in the USA. There was therefore considerable surprise when in 1982 they filed for bankruptcy. The company was totally viable but it had filed for bankruptcy owing to around 17,000 suits being filed against it in regard to its asbestos product lines. Many argued that Manville was acting in an illegal and immoral manner. In the event around 80 per cent of the company's equity was eventually used to compensate the many victims of its products. Manville had been killing people for years. What's more, they knew about it.

For more than 40 years, information had been reaching the company's medical department – and through it, the company' senior management – that something was wrong with the asbestos products they were producing. In particular, information implicating asbestos inhalation as a cause of asbestosis, a debilitating lung disease, as well as lung cancer and mesothelioma, an invariably fatal lung disease. In itself, this might not have been too shocking. However, rather than taking action Manville's managers suppressed the research. What is more, they apparently decided to conceal the information from both the affected employees and their customers. In 1952 Dr Kenneth Smith, the company's medical director, asked company executives to place a warning label on some asbestos products, which he felt could be dangerous to insulation workers. Their reply was they were in the business to provide jobs for people and make money for stockholders and the label might lose them sales. No labels were put on the products.

The depth of the issue became apparent when the case came to court. In one famous piece of testimony a lawyer recalled how 40 years earlier he had confronted Manville's corporate counsel about the company's policy of concealing chest X-ray results from employees. The lawyer had asked, 'Do you mean to tell me that you would let them work until they dropped dead?' The reply was 'Yes, we save a lot of money that way.'

Manville had clearly taken the view that it was cheaper to kill people than put warning labels on their goods. Amazingly, cases like these are by no means uncommon. The question that has to be asked of course is why?

Analysis

Perhaps the first thing we might ask is this. Were these people evil? I think that we can reject this view. First the Manville incident in particular happened over a long period of time – over 40 years. We cannot simply explain the issue in terms of the evil of a small number of people. The Electronics Company case too does not seem to have any particular evil attached to it either. The people who were involved were probably ordinary men and women, they found themselves in a dilemma and they solved it in a way that seemed least troublesome – not disclosing information that could hurt their product. The consequences probably never occurred to them at the time – although they probably thought about it later.

On the face of it, threatening the lives of customers and employees can make no sense in the long run. Why didn't the managers of these companies take the needs of these key stakeholders into account?

Ronald Green has suggested a number of reasons why this sort of thing might happen and these reasons are well worth considering:

1. A belief that the activity is within reasonable ethical and legal limits – that it is not really illegal or immoral. This is very much the 'it's OK, really' syndrome. We spoke before about pushing the line farther and farther. Very often it is this incrementalism that causes the problem. People rationalize that something is OK and so it becomes the norm and then some other problem come along and before they know it they have dug a huge hole for themselves. This is very clear with the Electronics Company case. At first, modifying

the parts was enough. When this did not work, they ended up testing these sophisticated parts on someone's gas oven! One wonders what they would have done next if this had not been enough. What seems to happen is that the goal seems to be the only thing that matters. Pressure turns us all into Machiavellian thinkers.

2. A conviction that the activity should be done because it is in the individual's or the corporation's best interests. The belief is that the person would be expected to do the action, even if on the face of it, it is immoral. Company loyalty is undoubtedly a key issue here. People feel that they have to do whatever is necessary to keep their companies going. Fear of losing your job is clearly part of this but cannot explain everything. It has been suggested that in modern life with the break-up of the extended family it is the organization that acts as most people's family. If this is true perhaps there is an inherent desire to keep your 'family' going? It is perhaps worth noting at this point that there is much evidence that employee loyalty is reducing. The reasons for this and their implications will be discussed later on in the book.

   What is clear is that top executives seldom ask their subordinates to do things that both of them know are against the law. But sometimes company leaders leave things unsaid that they don't really want to know about. In simple terms what is happening is that they are distancing themselves from their subordinates so that they don't get their hands dirty.

3. A view that the activity is safe because it will never be found out. 'We will never get caught, so why worry.' This is another common rationalization that people seem to fall for. They may well believe that even if it does come to light, they will have left the company a long time ago anyway. As we saw with the Manville case and the Libby one that is coming up, in some cases this view may be justified. The immoral act may take some time to come to light.

   Another problem is that often managers do not know when they have overstepped a mark until they have done it. It is not uncommon for ambitious managers to avoid costs by cutting corners in the short term to make themselves look good. Again, this relates to the problem of drawing the line, which we have already discussed.

4. A view that because the activity helps the company the company will support it and even protect the person who engages in it. Of course, as we have noted, this view is probably very misplaced!

There may be more to it than this, though. One idea that seems very relevant here is that of 'mass irresponsibility'. This is a concept that normally responsible people tend to act irresponsibly when they are part of a crowd. For example, let's assume that you are walking along a country lane, miles from anywhere and with nobody else around. You come across an old man who has fallen in the road. What do you do? Most people would help of course. Now put yourself in a major city such as London or New York. You walk along the crowded street and see the same old man lying in the gutter. Do you help him? Or do you simply rationalize that he is just some 'old bum' who will be looked after by someone else? The authorities will look after him; after all, you have better things to do! But this is the same old man. What has changed? Our willingness to walk away from responsibility when we are in a crowd may explain a lot.

Pause for thought ... Put this scenario to your colleagues or friends. What would they do? Why would they do what they say?

It might be thought that the Manville case was an isolated incident. It is not. More recently, a case was reported in *Mother Jones* that sounded very familiar. This is the Libby case:

CASE STUDY – **The Libby Case**

The case revolves around the valley town of Libby, Montana. It seems that mining company W. R. Grace & Company knew all along that asbestos from its Libby mine was making workers and their families sick and that many of their 12,000 workers were exposed to potentially dangerous conditions, but it kept it quiet.

As with the Manville case, for more than 40 years, an epidemic of lung disease spread through the valley. The main complaint was again asbestosis, along with malignant lung tumours and mesothelioma, a rare cancer of the pleural lining. The workers suspected a connection between their illnesses and the dust in the mine, but they could never be sure. Every day after work, the men would come home covered with a fine white powder. Their wives inhaled it as they scrubbed clothing and curtains and floors. Their children breathed it in as they played on the carpet. The miners were told it was just 'nuisance dust', nothing to worry about – even though W. R. Grace knew well that the dust they were breathing was loaded with microscopic asbestos fibres that could kill them and their families.

After their mother died in 1996, the Benefield family decided to sue W. R. Grace – only the second such lawsuit to be decided by a jury in Libby. As many as 70 other claims, filed following a 1986 court ruling permitting miners to sue Grace for damages, had been silently settled, with a gag order attached to the cash amount in each case.

Two years ago, a Libby jury – after hearing a Grace executive testify that he knew there was asbestos up in the mine, and that it could kill the mine workers and their families – awarded the family $250,000 in wrongful-death damages. But the verdict wasn't the wake-up call Benefield had hoped for. 'It didn't even make the local newspaper,' the family said.

This might seem strange. Why the lack of interest? Again, company loyalty seems to be the main factor. Libby was a mining town and it was accepted that the miners had a dangerous job that could sometimes result in bad health. Again, the town relied very heavily on the mine and blowing the whistle might well have resulted in closure and the loss of jobs.

After decades of neglect, the Environmental Protection Agency (EPA) finally started to investigate what was happening in Libby. In December 1999, an EPA emergency response team identified 33 asbestos deaths among Libby residents who had no occupational connection to the mine. 'With this number of cases, there's no doubt that the link here is the Libby mine,' said Paul Peronard, the EPA team leader. Asbestos in the mine led to asbestosis in the town – and all the signs pointed to W. R. Grace.

Interestingly enough, the workers were not mining asbestos. They were actually mining vermiculite. However, asbestos was present in the mine as a by-product and W. R. Grace's released some 5000 lbs or more of asbestos each day. On still days, some of it settled back on the mine site. When the wind blew from the east, a film of white dust covered the town. It was not uncommon for children to play in the dust and throw 'dust balls' at each other.

Bluffing and the Individual

One of the great problems with business bluffing is that it can put great pressure on the individual. An individual within a company often finds it difficult to adjust to the requirements of the business game. Often there is a conflict between the company and their ethics and this can cause considerable strain. We saw this in the example in Chapter 1 where the president of the company had to fire an ageing executive. As an individual, you would not want to get rid of the older person, but as a business person you know that you have to. Another example might be when you are asked to cheapen the quality of a well-established product in order to reduce costs or in some other way cut corners.

There is a lot of evidence and research to suggest that people suffer severe stress when asked to choose between the company and what they feel is ethical.

'It's Legal so it's OK!'

This is a common claim of business bluffers and it is indeed very easy to make this claim. After all, if the proposed action does not break the law of the land, how can it be wrong? Many of the actions that are being discussed in this book are not illegal in fact. How do we answer this? The ethics writer Richard George has put forward the following points, which are well worth our consideration:

1. Morality is broader than just legality. This is a key point. Laws do not and, realistically, cannot cover every aspect of our society. We can also point out that generally speaking, morals come first. Every law that exists was a moral once. It became a law because practice showed that a law had to be passed to restrict this immoral activity. It is also worth pointing out that members of the business community are also members of society. Just as individuals do not operate in a vacuum neither do businesses and as such they have responsibility to society.
2. The view that laws and not morals should restrict business practices fails to recognize two points:
   - One of the main reasons why things in this world are made illegal is because they are immoral.
   - If morals are not policed by industry then when laws do come along they end up being very punitive – very often it is far better for an industry to police itself than be policed. It is an interesting question to ask in the case of the Manville incident whether or not the action against both the company and the asbestos industry generally would have been so severe if Manville had put warning stickers on their products in the first place.

Does it Pay Not to Tell the Truth in Business?

We talked about the work of Kant in the first chapter. Kant suggested that a requirement of morality is consistency to action. If you said that discrimination against women was right then you should be willing to always state this, even if you were a woman yourself. This is an important point. Clearly many things in business require consistency of action. A good example of this is contracts. A contract is an agreement between two or more parties. It is usually enforceable by law for doing or not doing some stated thing. It is used in such areas as employment or credit warranty. What would happen if nobody honoured contracts of any form, every order went wrong, employees did not do as they were asked, and so on? Again we come back to Kant's idea of a universal rule. If everybody bluffed in business, we would have chaos. What makes it OK for some people to bluff in business? A good analogy is this: the traffic in cities like London is very congested and slow moving. Motorists are frequently asked whether or not they think that public transport was a good idea. Almost all will say that they think that more people should use public transport. But not *them* of course. By definition, business bluffing only works if the minority practises it.

Is Business Bluffing Wasteful?

There is much evidence to suggest this. For example, bluffing in pay negotiation between unions and management is normal. The management expects the union to demand a percentage pay increase it knows it won't get. The union expects that the management will say that their claim will force them to shut the business down. Such claims are never taken at face value and so both parties spend valuable time throwing unreasonable claims and counter claims at each other. Would a more open approach not be better?

Conclusion

We can conclude by saying that in truth business and life in general do not have precisely the same set of rules. However, the idea that it is acceptable to tell untruths in business 'because business is like that' is very dangerous. The business-bluffing concept is also dangerous. As we have seen, in extreme cases, it can kill people. Bluffing can also undermine the spirit of cooperation that is essential to business success. Success in business life is ultimately about cooperation and a lack of cooperation often leads to poor-quality products.

It can be argued that top management has a responsibility to exert a moral force within the company. Senior executives have to draw the line between loyalty and action against the laws and morals of society. What's more as things can go wrong the line has to be drawn well short of the point where people could claim that their rights had been violated.

CHAPTER 3

Is Capitalism a Just System?

According to a recent UN Development Programme study, the 200 richest people in the world have more income put together than the lowest 40 per cent of the population (or around 2.5 billion people). In addition, the top 20 per cent of the world's population earns 74 times as much per person as the bottom 20 per cent.

In this chapter, I want to look at the ethics of the capitalist system and its relationship with government. On the face of it, the answer to the question in the chapter title has to be 'yes'. After all, if you are studying at a business school or working in a commercial enterprise, the whole basis of what you do assumes the capitalist system to be justice. But is the system just and what is justice anyway? This chapter will attempt to answer this important question and consider some of the facts and issues in this key question.

What is Capitalism Anyway?

The term 'capitalist system' is widely used in business studies but its meaning is rarely explained. Before we look at the ethics of the system, we should try to define it. There seem to be a number of key areas that define the capitalist system:

Private ownership is usually seen as one of them although most capitalist economies have large amounts of public ownership. Perhaps the main thing in the definition is the fact that private ownership is widely accepted and available.

Competition is certainly a factor and many capitalist societies have formal systems that prevent competition becoming unfair.

All capitalist systems have the *profit motive* as a major building block. In theory at least, under capitalism earnings are unlimited. However, as we will see, the level of earnings available may vary a great deal and the justice of these earnings can be debated.

Many economists argue that the capitalist system in its purest sense is the only way that humanity progresses. Business, it can be argued, almost by definition needs freethinking. It can be argued that the free market is more than just about being free from an economic point of view. It can also be suggested that free can refer to the freedom of people being able to operate without coercion.

This brings us on to another aspect of capitalism. *Minimal government intervention* is usually put forward as a key feature. However, as we have seen, in many capitalist governments today this is not really true. Within all capitalist systems there is an emphasis on the management of the economy through taxation, public expenditure, and so on. Some countries may well have a welfare state. In addition, the market may be distorted by the use of state aid for ailing industries and other subsidies.

It must be said that there are many supporters of the capitalist system who would not support interventionism and we will discuss the views of some of these individuals shortly.

Having said this, in recent times the amount of state intervention has been reduced with a drive towards privatization and deregulation, particularly in the UK under the Conservative government of Margaret Thatcher.

This minimal intervention is often known as the *laissez-faire* approach. An extreme form of this would argue that the role of government should be restricted to protection of property, the enforcement of contract and the upholding of rules of fair competition.

An interesting question is this: Is democracy an aspect of capitalism? The fact that we have had capitalist societies without it should suggest not. However, this is not a clear-cut question because defining what democracy is is not straightforward either. Consider the following:

> President Bill Clinton announced in 1997 that following the thawing of the cold war, more than half of the world's population – 54.8% by his reckoning – was now democratic. However, there have been many cases of free and fair elections that have not produced the sort of democracy that Thomas Jefferson was talking about. Many governments have had free and fair elections that would not be acceptable in other parts of the world and, there are elected governments that offer few human rights. It can be argued that some aspects of the US government system are not democratic in the strict sense either. The US senate is generally believed to be the most undemocratic upper house in the world – if you exclude the

> UK House of Lords. Every state sends two senators to Washington regardless of population. Thus Wyoming, with 481000 inhabitants has the same voice in senate as California with 31 million. A single senator can hold up almost any bill, which can thwart the majority and bring government to deadlock.
>
> *Fareed Zakaria*, Newsweek, *29 December/5 January 1998*

There is one other key area of capitalism of course; the idea that capitalism employs labour. The providers of labour are responsible to the providers of capital. This fact in itself raises a number of questions for discussion:

Is Capitalism a Just System?

It can be argued that capitalism is the only system that safeguards the freedom of the independent mind and recognizes the sanctity of the individual. Certainly the rapid improvements in the standard of living of most people have come about as a result of capitalism. However, this does not necessarily mean that the system is just. Perhaps the best place to start is to ask the question, what do we mean by justice?

Justice is really about the morally proper treatment of people – *being fair and giving people what they deserve.*

There are actually many forms of justice but in this case the real issue is distributive justice. People getting the financial rewards that they deserve given the labours that they put in.

Does the Capitalist Society Have Distributive Justice?

The central argument around this is the fact that there is an unequal distribution of wealth in capitalist societies. Although this varies there is always inequality.

Let us take a model of a 'typical' capitalist society. This does not refer to any particular country but would be a reasonable description of a country, say, in Western Europe. Let us start with incomes first of all. In a country like this, a substantial minority will receive incomes which fall significantly below the mean average for the population as a whole. These people may find it difficult to live on a day-to-day basis and may well be in receipt of help from the government. This group will include low-skill workers, people living on a state pension and the unemployed. The majority of the people will be around the average for incomes. Above this, a small minority will have anything up to several times the average income. These might be the professional members of our society – senior managers, doctors, and so on. Beyond this, a tiny minority decreasing in number as their income increases will exceed the average by much more, by tens or even hundreds, and in rare cases even thousands. These will be the most successful businesspeople and people with extraordinary earnings such as footballers and film stars. Because the distribution is so weighted towards the top a majority will receive less than the mean average. However, we should note that under capitalism income levels are reasonably evenly split.

What About the Distribution of Wealth Rather Than Income?

Here the picture changes a great deal. Under most capitalist societies, someone who is not earning an average income will have very little wealth indeed. They will probably live in rented accommodation or with their family and have few possessions. Those around average income and a few times above will probably have a fair degree of wealth. However, most of this will not be very marketable. For most people their home will be their main store of capital. Given that they have to live somewhere, clearly this is a very inflexible source of wealth. Those at the top end will have a great deal more wealth and what's more it will be far more marketable, perhaps in the form of businesses, land stocks, shares, and so on.

It is worth noting that this fact has an impact on incomes. Those with the very highest incomes will probably gain it from their possession of wealth rather than from their work. Rock stars like David Bowie and Paul McCartney will make a significant amount of their income not from music but from the investments that they have made over the years. (Bowie has even set up an Internet bank bearing his name!)

The difference between the very top and the rest is clearly significant. Indeed, it can be argued that most capitalist societies, even the most evenly distributed, basically consist of the rich and the rest.

However, this does not really answer the question: Is capitalism just? We have so far only explained how the system works.

Wealth and Power

Wealth is not the only factor. The power that this wealth gives is also a factor in the justice equation. There is an obvious correlation between the degrees of wealth and the degrees of power, with the rich having most power and the poor having the least. This tends to create an enormous concentration of power. What's more, in capitalism you have a large degree of control resting with the owners of enterprises, which again means that it is the rich who hold power. Is it just that the true power in society is only held by a very few people?

Opponents to this situation argue that this is wrong because there should be a more even distribution of wealth and power.

Capitalism and Distributive Justice

CASE STUDY – **The English Premier League**

A recent study, the largest ever survey of professional footballers in the UK, showed that the average pay of England's top footballers is nearly £8000 a week – more than ten times that of players at the bottom of the Football League. The average basic salary for Premiership players over the age of 20 has risen to £409,000 a year.

Some 36 per cent of players in the same age group earn more than £500,000 a year and 9 per cent of Premiership footballers – about 100 – earn more than £1 million a year. Manchester United captain Roy Keane, in the 1999/2000 season, won a long-standing battle with his club to become the country's highest paid player on £52,000 a week.

At the other end of the pay scale, players and trainees aged 17–20 earn between £19,000 and £45,000 a year on average.

When questioned, Professional Footballers' Association chairman Barry Horne said: 'Compared to golfers, tennis players and others within the wider world of entertainment, footballers' salaries are not astronomical.'

At the same time most nurses in the National Health Service earn less than £20,000 per annum. Many earn far less than this. How can the disparity between the footballers and the nurses be explained? However, compared with really high earners the footballers are paupers. The golfer Tiger Woods is reputed now to be the highest earning athlete in the world. He is on course (as of July 2000) to have earned more than $6 billion throughout his career. This income is made up of substantial prize money added to a variety of endorsements from companies such as Nike, American Express and Rolex.

Perhaps the most famous high earner of them all is Bill Gates. Gates's wealth varies with the share price of Microsoft but is clearly considerable. It was recently calculated that a National Health nurse would need to work 100,000 years to catch up with the chairman of Microsoft.

How Can This Difference Be Justified?

One big issue is the question of the link between distributive justice and equality. Those who see a more or less close correlation are known as egalitarians. A more qualified view might be that society should provide at least a minimum level for its citizens although it is perfectly acceptable to have as much as you like at the top.

Another equality argument is that equal shares are acceptable, providing people themselves are equal. If we all make an equal contribution to society then we should all get the same.

The Service Argument

Most economists explain the capitalist system in terms of the service argument. This suggests that the wealth an individual receives from the capitalist system is directly related to the service that they put into society. Service is made up of a simple equation, which takes into account the supply or rarity of whatever is being offered, the demand for it and the number of people who are enjoying the service. Thus Bill Gates and his company have served countless millions around the world and Microsoft has relatively little competition. Premier League footballers give tremendous service in that they attract large numbers of people to their grounds. In addition, far more people watch them on the TV and the TV companies are prepared to pay huge sums of money for the privilege of screening their matches. At the same time, to complete the equation, there are relatively few people on the planet who have the skills of the Premier League players. So these people have high demand skills that are in very short supply. Inevitably the price of these footballers – or Bill Gates – will rise and that explains why they earn so much. On the other hand, whilst the nurses perform an excellent and highly worthwhile job, there are far more people capable of doing the work. Despite the low pay, many people are prepared to do the work for a low rate because of their commitment and the job satisfaction that it gives. Essentially the demand is less strong and the supply far greater. This must result in a lower price for the commodity and inevitably the wages of nurses are far lower than Premiership footballers.

Supporters of the capitalist system argue that it is just that – a system. It is a predictable set of rules that will work for you every time if you play according to these rules. However, this brings us on to the next question.

Does Capitalism Reward Merit?

Not always or everywhere. People can fail in business through no fault of their own. They can be rich because of inheritance or because they were unscrupulous or just plain lucky. In these cases the service argument tends to fall down. These people, unlike the footballers or Mr Gates, have not really contributed heavily to society. People can also be made poor through illness or misfortune.

There is also not always a correlation between skill, dedication and rewards. There are many cases of people putting tremendous skill and effort into worthwhile causes yet ending up not being paid. They can make outstanding contributions and get nothing. Others of far less talent can make vast fortunes.

How *Much* Inequality Should There Be?

One interesting way of answering this question is to take some international comparisons. Economists when they look at a countries' spread of income take the top fifth and the bottom fifth and compare the ratio between the two:

The very successful and stable Scandinavian countries have ratios around 4:0.
In highly successful Japan the ratio is 4:3.
In the UK, 6:8.
In the USA, 8:9.
In Brazil, which is generally held to be the extreme example of the world, the ratio is 26:1. It has been estimated that if the ratio could be reduced to 5, the bottom fifth of the Brazilian population would see a ten-fold rise in living standards.

A key feature we can note is the massive spread of this top fifth. What we are talking about is the average for the top fifth. The range within the top fifth can be ten or hundred times that of the people in the bottom half of this top fifth. Many developing nations have tiny numbers of very wealthy people with the majority of their populations living in poverty.

Is there a correlation between stability and spread? Undoubtedly there is. The most countries, such as those in Scandinavia, tend to have relatively low income splits. This reflects the sophistication of their populations, with relatively few low-skill, low-income people and also a policy of redistributive justice, which reduces the extremes of income and wealth. Can there be too much of a split between rich and poor? These figures suggest that there can.

Should Anyone Earn That Much Money?

The capitalist system may well produce some very wealthy people, but does anyone really need that much money? It can be argued that such huge earnings are just plain wrong. Motivation is often put forward as an argument for these huge discrepancies. It could be suggested that a shopfloor worker could be motivated to become a senior executive if they had the possibility of a five-fold increase, but does this executive need a ten-fold or twenty-fold increase to motivate them to get to the top of a major corporation? Would a rather more modest increase do the job?

A good example of this occurred during the 1992 visit of US President George Bush to Japan (when he was rather a sick man, so that it is often known as the Vomit Tour). Bush took with him the chief executives of the three largest American motor companies. They aimed to remove the restrictions on the export of Japanese cars to the USA. The force of the plea was somewhat blunted when it was pointed out that the Japanese managers of the much more successful car companies were paid only around tenth that of their American counterparts. To put this in perspective, Lee Iaccoca was being paid $4.5 million a year at the time. Of course, Iaccoca had been the saviour of Chrysler and had achieved great things. But can this level of pay be justified all the same?

Clearly it can be argued that extremes like this are likely ultimately to have negative results. These negative results might include resentment at the lower levels of society by the poor who express their resentment by turning to crime.

At the same time, those in the middle of society can feel frustrated in some cases where the rich who perhaps know the right person block the route to the top. It is often said that getting on in society is not about what you know or how good you are; it is about who you know.

There is also an argument that there is inefficiency in this society because of the wealth, which goes into inheritance rather than as incentives to work hard and progress.

CASE STUDY – **Singapore: A 'Fine' Society**

Its inhabitants often describe Singapore as being a 'fine' society. There is a fine for this, a fine for that, a fine for everything! Although possibly an exaggeration, there is some truth in this assertion. Littering attracts a heavy fine – up to $1000 Singapore, which is around $500 US; smoking is banned from all public buildings (and 'public' means private shops and restaurants); and you cannot eat, drink or smoke on public transport. A recent law made it an offence not to flush a public toilet. This was resolved by putting automatic flushing mechanisms on toilets. Urinating in the lifts of public housing was a problem, so close-circuit TV and ammonia detectors were installed so that security staff could catch culprits red-handed. Chewing and bubble gum are illegal substances (although visitors may bring it in for personal use: offering it to a resident is seen as a form of pushing).

Singapore has around three million people on a tiny island, so pollution due to car exhausts could be a problem. It isn't, because Singapore is the only country in the world that rations car usage by massive taxation on car purchases and by selling the right to use a car by public auction. Buying a car in Singapore is more like buying a house elsewhere in the world, in terms of cost. Accordingly, only the very well-off have cars. Further costs for motorists have been added in recent years by systems of road pricing.

Freedom of speech has some limits, criticism of the government is not encouraged, and the penalties for crimes can be very severe. For hard-drug traffickers, the penalty is death.

Yet Singapore has the highest standard of living in Asia, second only to Japan in per capita income. Economic growth rates over the past decade have been impressive, several times that achieved by European countries or the USA. Even the Far Eastern crisis seems to have been ridden out well. Unemployment rates are low and state support for business is generally very strong.

The streets are immaculate, and free from any signs of poverty, and all sectors of society seem well cared for. Crime is minimal and the city-state's streets are amongst the safest in the world. Public transport is cheap, clean, plentiful and safe.

Question: Singapore is often described as being the Switzerland of Asia, reflecting its wealth despite natural resources, and lifestyle; but are the government measures justified to achieve a stable society, or is this just government intervention gone mad?

Capitalism and State Intervention: The Views of Nozick and Tracinski

The Singapore case shows how a government can intervene in society and engineer it in certain directions. In this section we will consider some alternative views on state intervention. So far we have talked about the question of redistributive justice and how having too great a disparity in society can create social problems. This would suggest a need for the state to intervene. Supporters of the capitalist system would argue that there are, if anything, too many controls in society as it is.

An example of this might be the work of Robert Nozick. Nozick's view is known as the entitlement view of social justice. Nozick argues that the possession of property is an inviable human right. Any attempt by government is thus a violation of human rights. The only condition that Nozick puts down is that the property must be justly possessed. This means that no force or fraud was used.

Nozick would therefore argue that those people who argue that people should be given more equality through government action would be wrong because this redistribution of wealth would be forcible and therefore violate people's rights. It would violate the rights of the rich to their property unless they agreed to forgo the property without argument. From this it can be clearly argued that capitalism is just and that any attempt to change capitalism must be unjust.

Robert Tracinski puts forward a similar view. Tracinski argues that capitalism in its purest form is the only acceptable form of economic and social system. It might be argued that capitalism is a very practical system but one that is inherently immoral. Tracinski argues against this. He suggests that capitalism is moral because of its practicality. Capitalism lets people think on their own without the outside interference of a large state machine. Capitalism is the result of the combined thinking of thousands of individual thinkers. Capitalism is often put forward as being the survival of the fittest. Those who have the most power and energy will make it. However, Tracinski suggests, students of Darwin will point out that he was not talking about fitness in an energy sense at all, but in the sense that certain life forms will thrive because they most fit the environment in which they live. It can be said that capitalism works in the same way. Under capitalism we are all freethinkers and it is those with the ideas that have the most successful thinking who will make the most money. It is easy to decry wealthy individuals such as Bill Gates of Microsoft for their huge wealth. However, as we have said, Gates and his company have come up with ideas that have served many millions of people.

What is wrong with state intervention? Tracinski argues that in a state-regulated society it is the state bureaucrats that make the decisions. The freethinking of individuals is reduced and apathy tends to occur. Capitalism can thus be said to be more practical because under capitalism, people will have incentives. They will tend to work harder, longer and smarter. They will also be much more likely to take risks, because the potential return will be greater. Why take a risk if there is little benefit?

Above all, Tracinski suggests that capitalism is practical because it is based on self-interest. Capitalism is just because it respects and gives power to the individual. It assumes that everyone is a freethinking spirit. If it is morally right for individuals to be free, then capitalism is just.

What About the Welfare State?

Both Tracinski and Nozick argue that rather than being a deliverer of social justice, the welfare state represents a gross injustice in society. The reason for this, they argue, is as follows. They picture the welfare state as a system that steals money from the majority of citizens to give it to others on the basis that those with more wealth have a duty to serve those with less.

The problem with this, they suggest, is that the welfare state creates more problems than it solves. There is a danger, they argue, that rather than 'helping up' the people who need it, it actually creates a new underclass of dependent citizens. These people, they suggest, are often quite capable of looking after themselves but choose not to do so because it is easier not to work. What is more, the welfare state along with the minimum wage arrangement tends to create so-called poverty traps, where it is financially more viable for people to stay at home rather than work. It can also be pointed out that the standard of living in most countries of the world has risen dramatically over the years and much of this is down to the capitalist system. They accept that there will always be a small number of people who cannot support themselves, but it can be argued that this group will reduce if a more capitalist society comes about. Those who are left can be supported by private charities.

This may appear a rather harsh view to many. Should society really be based on the survival of the fittest – or is that really the fairest and most equitable way?

Conclusion

So is capitalism a just system? Perhaps we might conclude this chapter with the following thoughts. Capitalism has without doubt shown itself to be a successful system for creating wealth. Other systems such as socialism have clearly failed in this respect. However, whilst this cannot be doubted, it is in the distribution of this wealth where we have to be a little more critical. Can we really justify a footballer earning nearly as much in a week as a nurse gets in a year? Economists will, as we have seen, justify this on the grounds of service. However, is that the only basis on which our society should run?

Perhaps the best conclusion we can come to is this. Capitalism is far from perfect, but it is probably the best system that has been developed so far. That said, it does seem to need some modification from its purest form if we are to ensure stability and social order – even though some economists would argue that point. However, capitalism is merely a reflection of our choices expressed through the economic system. Footballers get paid more than nurses because the citizens of the world believe that and express it through purchasing power. If you find that decision unreasonable, perhaps you should question the priorities of society rather than the capitalist system as such.

CHAPTER 4

Employees and Rights

This chapter looks at the relationship between the workplace and human rights. First we will look at some of the key issues in workplace rights generally and then talk about some of the more specific areas encountered.

To start with, it is important to make a distinction between two main types of rights. On the one hand we have ethical rights that we might call justice or correctness. These are the sorts of rights that we spoke about in the previous chapter. In addition to this we have legal rights, which are given in the law of the land. These are usually a lot more straightforward because we can look in the relevant statute books to gain guidance as to what our rights are and disputes can be resolved in courts of law.

It is relatively easy, at least in principle, to determine what legal rights a citizen has. Human rights, on the other hand, are more difficult to determine. Human rights are supposed to apply irrespective of where we have been born, or any legislation, which has been enacted. Examples of human rights might include freedom of speech, freedom of thought, and so on.

Pause for thought ... Ask some of your friends or colleagues what they regard as their human rights. How do these compare with legal rights?

A key point is that for a right to exist it must *be a practical possibility.* It would be nice if we all had Ferraris but realistically, giving everyone in the world the right to have a Ferrari would not be very practical!

A human right has to be universal. You cannot have a situation where you have a human right that applies to one person and not another. Perhaps the best source of information on human rights is the UN Declaration. The United Nations Declaration on Human Rights declares that all men (strangely it does not mention women) are free and equal in rights. These rights include food, shelter, and other basic requirements of life. Most people would find this acceptable if asked, and many of the answers that you received from the 'pause for thought' might well have been along these lines. A problem though is that in the workplace we also have work specific rights. These might include a right to a pay cheque of a certain size, or the right to use certain facilities. In an earlier chapter we asked if we should treat life in general and business differently. There can be no doubt that rights in the workplace are very different from rights elsewhere. Some of these may well be acceptable to us, but some may not and we might well ask if our rights are compromised too much when we join an organization. Very often, we may find ourselves in a quandary. We have a moral view that is at odds with the organization that we have a contract with. What do we do then? Where does our loyalty lie?

The basic problem for those who wish to impose a fair non-discriminatory policy within the work place is this. How can you say that 'everyone has equal rights in the workplace' when clearly that cannot be possible? How can someone have free speech if that means a right to insult the boss? When it comes to the crunch, someone has to be in charge. In the workplace, the old adage 'we are all equal, but some people are more equal than others' seems to apply!

The Right to Work

This is a very problematic area. The United Nations Declaration of Human Rights states that 'Everyone has the right to work, a free choice of employment, to just and favourable conditions of work, and to protection against unemployment.' This is very laudable, but the Declaration does not make it clear *who* is supposed to make sure that this happens.

Clearly, we cannot have a situation where a worker turns up at a company at random asking for a job on the grounds that they are a human being and therefore have a 'right to work'. Perhaps it might be down to government to uphold this right. Certainly some socialist systems provided an almost guaranteed right to work. The former Soviet

Union was perhaps a good example of this. However, this proved inefficient (there were cases in the former Soviet Union of three people delivering the milk – one to drive, one to carry the milk and one to open the gate!) and is also very interventionist. As we have seen, we might argue that too much government intervention is not a good thing.

Perhaps the right to work means something different to this. What is perhaps more reasonable is the view that everyone has a right to *offer* themselves for employment and be treated fairly when they do so. A government that imposed an employment ban on married women, or who restricted the jobs that a certain religious group could apply would definitely be in breach of the article.

There have been many instances of this 'right to work' being compromised in the past. In the UK during the 1970s there was considerable use made of the 'closed shop'. This is where an employer forms an agreement with a trade union whereby the employer only recognizes one union and bargains only with them. In return the employer agrees that all of its workers should join this union. Refusal to join could result in dismissal for the employee. Effectively, employees could be forced to join the union against their will. This would seem to be a good example of influencing the right to work. The 'closed shop' has become far more difficult to achieve since the Thatcher era, although single union agreements are still quite common.

It is often argued that in the USA, citizens have had freedom of assembly, press, speech, in homes and churches since the country was founded, but once a worker walks through the door of work then the whole scene changes. Certainly there are cases in some businesses where some of these freedoms have been increased but this is very dependent on the president of the company and they may change. Often 'freedoms' are quickly revoked when the company starts running into trouble. It can be argued that many Western nations are a paradox, one rule for living and one rule for working. This fits in rather well with the 'business bluffing' idea and the views of Weber and others.

Pause for thought ...
Sit down with some colleagues and ask them what freedoms and rights they feel that they have given up by working. How reasonable do they feel these are? After all, they have signed a contract with their employer and it might be thought fair that they give up some of their freedom as an individual. Or is it the case that we are all 'wage slaves' as is often suggested? If so, is that morally acceptable?

Equality of Opportunity

The Declaration goes on to state that everyone, without discrimination, has the right to equal pay for equal work. Differentials must be justified. This applies both to employment policy and wage differentials. If we appoint applicant A rather than applicant B then we have to be able to justify that selection. In the UK, the Race Relations Act and the Sex Discrimination Act require that personnel departments have to have a relevant reason for refusing to employ a black person or a woman (or indeed any other race colour or sex.) Being black or a woman is not deemed to be relevant – apart from in some very specific exceptions such as in certain ethnic restaurants.

There are other areas in the UK where discrimination is still common. Age, religion, class, political affiliation, physical appearance, and to a large extent disability are all examples where discrimination does go on. If you accept that the sole criteria for employing someone is the ability to do the job, then this cannot be morally right.

A good example that we might look at is the question of age discrimination. In the USA, the Age Discrimination in Employment Act (ADEA) of 1967 has made it illegal to discriminate in employment on the grounds of age. The thought process behind the Act was very straightforward. It was becoming clear that older workers were both finding it hard to stay in jobs and to find new work if they lost a previous one. This showed itself in the form of above average levels of unemployment in older workers. Furthermore it was felt that age discrimination, which is totally arbitrary and has no relationship to the skill involved generally speaking, has a long-term negative effect on business generally. In simple terms some very good people were being needlessly wasted. The Act was designed to improve the employment prospects of older people, and for people to be hired on the basis of ability rather than age.

The Act prevents employers discriminating either in employment or in recruitment for people who are over the age of 40. Furthermore they cannot categorize older people (you cannot say that a certain job is a 'young person's job', for example).

The Act covers most aspects of human-resources management including apprenticeship programmes, job advertisements, pre-employment enquiries, and benefits. The last case is an interesting one. The Older Workers Benefits Act of 1990 amended the ADEA to make it illegal for employers to deny benefits to older employees. The only exception to this is where the cost of the benefit increases for older people. For example, life insurance will generally increase for older people. In this case you can reduce the benefit, but only to the point where the amount spent is the same for all employees. In other words you are not expected to spend more on benefits for older workers, just no less.

What About Employer Rights?

This is an interesting and rather controversial area. Equal opportunity is a concept that is accepted by many but it also has its critics. Don't employers have rights too? Surely they have a right to decide who works for them? You might argue it like this. We have in most democratic countries freedom of contract. If I am an entrepreneur, I can buy and sell whatever I want to whom I want. Now, employment is a form of contract of supply, so surely I have every right to employ who I want without question?

If I don't like working alongside black people or women or practising Christians, then should I not have a right to do something about that? Many of the economists that we have been discussing might also argue that equality of opportunity is just yet another example of government intervention in the market system.

> Pause for thought ...
> I once knew a man who ran a sales organization. He was convinced from past experience that women made much better sales people than men. For this reason, he went out of his way to hire women and avoided hiring men, even though many applied. He would argue that he was not being discriminatory. Merely, he was doing the best for his business. What would you say to him?

The basic problem is that rights do have a habit of conflicting, and what we really have in the 'pause for thought' is a question of relative importance. There needs to be a trade-off. Is the welfare of the minority group of workers, who find it hard to gain employment, to be limited by this presumed right of employers to employ who they want?

Another argument put forward by the *laissez-faire* school – including economists like Friedman – is that if the only real aim of the company is to make profits then anything which goes against this has got to be a bad thing. Taking the argument of the sales manager in the 'pause for thought', surely you should hire people who are most likely to get the best result for the organization irrespective of what type of person they are.

> Pause for thought ...
> Consider what we have discussed about the aims of the capitalist system and society in general. Which do you think is more

important, employer rights or employee rights? If hiring whom you want makes the most money, would it not be better for society to have no discrimination laws? Where does that leave the most vulnerable in society?

Affirmative Action

This is another controversial area. The basic thinking of affirmative action is very straightforward. The view is taken that in the past certain groups have been disadvantaged in some way. Women, certain racial and ethnic groups and so forth have been disadvantaged in some way. In order to overcome this inequality, some argue that there should be a policy of affirmative action. Affirmative action involves the recognition that certain groups of individuals have been discriminated against in the past and tries to 'redress the balance'. This may involve special schemes to assist disadvantaged groups, and positive discrimination. Positive discrimination may involve the setting of quotas for disadvantaged groups or it may simply involve letting the employee's gender, race or sexual orientation tip the scales when an appointment or promotion is being made. In simple terms, if a 'disadvantaged' individual and a 'non-disadvantaged' individual of equal ability come up for a job, the disadvantaged individual should be appointed. The advantage of this is seen as two-fold. First, by appointing the disadvantaged candidate, you are redressing the years of discrimination that such people have experienced. Secondly, if more people from this group are appointed then it will become more common for this type of person to be in this profession. They will become more accepted and the discrimination will reduce.

There may be much to merit this, but there is also a problem. What happens if you are not one of the disadvantaged? If you have the 'misfortune' to be white and male (in a typical Western society) is it really your fault that there has been prejudice in the past? Why should *you* pay?

Affirmative action policies are clearly controversial. Employers who actively discriminate towards certain groups can of course be accused of discrimination – the very thing that they are supposed to be trying to avoid. If it is right to appoint someone on merit, what is the difference between appointing someone because they are a woman than because they are a man?

There is also a strong argument that affirmative action does not serve the disadvantaged groups. This is because people in these groups who gain employment may be charged of getting the job only because of the affirmative policy and not on merit. What is more, it may become apparent that they have worse performance than those who might have been appointed by more traditional methods, reinforcing the prejudice (for example) that women are less effective workers. Many women's groups suggest that in situations where there is clear prejudice against women, such as certain selling jobs, the sex discrimination act does women no favours because in that situation it is suggesting that women should be appointed even though they are not as suited as men.

One argument is that since there are certain 'niche' occupations where women (for example) have still to gain a foothold, and would seem to have been disadvantaged irrespective of legislation, then positive discrimination will iron this out. For example in the UK it has always been noted that there are very few women science teachers. This relative absence might well influence children and convince them that physics is a male subject. Attracting women into physics teaching might help redress the balance and provide role models for girls to go into the sciences.

Clearly these facts are only viable if they are stopped when equality is arrived at. Many women's groups have argued that affirmative action is acceptable but only as a short-term measure of redress.

Another suggestion that has been put forward is that of quota schemes. Rather than letting gender, race or disability tip the scales, firms can allocate pre-determined percentages of the total work force to certain categories and either make appointments accordingly or at least aim to bring the workforce up to this level in due course. This concept has been particularly common in government and state-run industries. As with many ideas for eliminating or reducing discrimination, quota schemes are not without their problems. They can lead to situations where appointment is made not on merit but on the basis that the quota has to be made up. This again leaves the appointee with the same problem of the positive discrimination. They only got the job 'because of the system' will be a common complaint. Of course, this may not be true, but it is a stigma that workers from these groups will have to deal with. The quota system can also by definition discriminate against applicants who do not fall into the protected categories. Also there may be some categories of disadvantaged who do not fit into any group. To cite one example, the Indian government has had a policy for reserving certain posts for scheduled castes in government jobs and the universities. This has made it much harder for certain Indian minority groups such as Jains and Parsees who fall outside the caste system. The basic problem is that they are not Hindus and thus now have to compete for a reduced number of jobs and higher education places with everybody else who is not a scheduled caste.

The Concept of Fair Wages

The UN Declaration on Human Rights says that 'Everyone who works has the right to just and favourable remuneration, ensuring for himself and his family an existence worthy of human dignity and supplemented if necessary by other means of social protection.'

The most obvious differentiation amongst workers is earnings. As we have previously noted, the remuneration paid to the people in the world varies a great deal and its fairness or not is very much a matter of opinion. What is 'just and fair remuneration' anyway? The concept is not easy to put into practice.

Trade Unions, the UN Declaration and Human Rights

Article 23 of the Declaration states that 'Everyone has the right to form and to join trade unions for the protection of his interests.' This right stems from the right of peaceful assembly and association. The Declaration also states that no one may be compelled to belong to an association. We have already mentioned closed shops and single-union agreements. It would seem that these violate the concept of the UN Declaration. Further, it can be argued that all members of a trade union gain the benefits of a collective bargaining, not simply those who belong to the union. Is it not unfair that those who do not pay subscriptions should receive equal benefits to those who do? If this is the case, should people be forced to join a union?

Those who support opting out will appeal to the individual freedom. Surely workers have the right to determine who shall represent their interests, or whether they will not bother with representation all together. Finally, those employers who wish to abolish the closed shop could simply be accused of being union busters or trying to place workers at the mercy of the market.

Do the Rules for Security and Privacy Differ Between Home and the Workplace?

When you go home you have well-established rights to protection from arbitrary search in the form of search warrants, and in some countries, such as the USA, these rights are very strong. The laws of the land will protect you from any invasion of privacy. However, your rights in the workplace are far more limited, generally speaking. As a rule, employers can search lockers, desks, and so on with only a 'reasonable belief' that you have carried out some wrong action. Is this fair? Is it acceptable that people forgo a right of privacy when they enter the workplace? You might think so. However, many employers will tell you that they usually pick up wrongdoing by employees when the employee goes away on holiday.

Pause for thought ...
In an example known to the author, one individual had taken around £100,000 of goods and money from an employer. This was only discovered because the employer had searched their possessions at work when they were away. Was the employer right to do what they did in this case?

Employer Rights Revisited

Where does this take us from the point of view of employer rights? The fact that most workers have a contract of employment and many a definite job description suggests that employees have legal and contractual obligations to carry out certain tasks. This, above all, suggests loyalty.

But what happens when there is a conflict between the contractual obligations of a worker and their moral conscience? What happens if your company is carrying out something that is immoral in your view but not illegal? Because it is not illegal you cannot call the police in. Should you tell someone? Do you, as a citizen of the world, have a moral obligation to do so? If the answer is yes to that, whom do you tell? Your boss, or the papers perhaps? Your boss might be in on the deal – the last person you want to tell. On the other hand, telling the papers can be very destructive for the company. Do you want to be that destructive? What happens if the company is guilty but either way goes bust and puts 1000 people out of work? Do you want the misfortune of all these people on your conscience? One overarching view that might be put here is that you should always fulfil your contract once you had signed it irrespective of your moral views. After all, if you refuse then some other person is going to have to comply. The action will happen eventually and the result will be the same so what's the point anyway?

Whistleblowing

A more difficult situation is that of whistleblowing. This occurs when an individual goes public with some information – usually company confidential information – because they believe that what the company is doing is immoral or otherwise wrong. Sissela Bok defines whistleblowers as persons who 'sound an alarm from within the very organization in which they work, aiming to spotlight neglect or abuses that threaded the public interest'. This is a good definition. The whistleblower is faced with a very difficult moral decision. The issue may be very serious, as we mentioned in the Manville case in Chapter 2, but the consequences could also be great. The whistleblower may face dismissal or worse. Whistle-blowing is not just routine gossip. The important thing about it is that the whistleblower perceives his actions as making a protest that is in the public interest. He or she is making a protest that is above his/her own level of interest and in the interest of the people.

Another problem that has to be considered is how do you know if you have all of the facts? Are you making your decision to blow the whistle on solid grounds? What happens if you are not and a lot of innocent people loose their jobs because of you?

Whistleblowers go public because they believe that they have a good story. Many things that happen in the workplace may be important but have very limited public interest. The whistleblower is usually going to the press because they firmly believe that there is a story there. One big danger of this is that the whole thing grows out of proportion. The ability of the press to sensationalize stories is well known.

Yet another concern is the issue of public trust. Whistleblowing can create tremendous concern and a belief that everyone is corrupt. This is especially true in the case of the public whistleblower.

Let us consider the issue of who should you tell. In many cases of whistleblowing, the people around the whistleblower were very frustrated by the fact that the person did not talk to them first before 'going public'. This returns us to the loyalty issue one more. Of course, it is easy for the whistleblower to retort that they could not go to the boss because the chances are that the boss was involved in the first place and might just ignore the problem or cover his or her tracks.

All of this assumes that the whistleblower goes public. Sometimes, whistleblowing may be internal – although it often becomes public in the end. A recent example happened in the UK in July 2000 when an accountant named Antonio Fernandez was dismissed from his £70,000 a year job after telling the US directors of his company that his boss had taken £370,000 in unsubstantiated expenses out of the business. The money had been used on a range of extravagant items including Caribbean holidays. In the event, the UK management of his company asked Fernandez to resign. When he refused, he was dismissed. In the event, Fernandez was awarded £293,000 compensation and his UK boss was asked to pay back a substantial amount of the money that he had appropriated.

Another interesting point put forward by many thinkers is this one. What makes the whistleblower so righteous anyway? Sometimes the whistleblower may be a junior person, as in the famous Sarah Tisdall case. However, very often they are senior people who are part of the very corporate culture that is supposedly so rotten. Should a senior manager 'show their dirty washing' in public, especially when they might have dirtied it in the first place? The impact on morale could be very serious, as we have noted.

One thing *is* certain. There is really little protection for employees who object to carrying out immoral, unethical or illegal orders from their superiors. Certainly you can resign, but this may not be a very satisfactory solution, because the loser is you. We might note that whistleblowing is on the increase. There are many reasons for this, but the openness of modern business, the improvements in communications, and the reduced loyalty that modern employment practices have brought about all play a part.

How might whistleblowing be addressed? Whistleblowing would be less likely if the companies were more open. The main reason why a whistleblower acts is because they believe that something is going on in the company that should not be. Revealing it may have a number of effects, including creating a climate of suspicion amongst the people in that company, even if in fact there is no problem. If a company is up front about its actions then the whistleblower may have less to be concerned about.

Is whistleblowing acceptable? We might conclude that there will be times when the blowing of the whistle to halt wrongdoing is a good thing. Some of the classic cases in this book tend to support this view rather well. However, it does not mean to say that whistleblowing is *always* good. Whether or not you accept the loyalty argument or not, blowing the whistle is likely to have a major impact on the stakeholders of the business irrespective of what is proved and it is not an action that we should take lightly. Perhaps the best conclusion is to encourage an ethical culture in an organization such that there is no need for whistleblowing in the first place.

Sexual Harassment

There are many definitions of sexual harassment. Essentially, it involves such things as unwanted sexual advances, requests for sexual favours and other verbal or physical conduct of a sexual nature within the workplace. Most writers would agree that there are three main forms of sexual harassment, as follows:

1. Harassment related to employment conditions. This is when submission to such sexual conduct is made explicitly or implicitly a term or condition of an individual's employment. In other words, if

the person does not do as the (perhaps senior) person requires, they may lose their job.

2. Harassment related to employment consequences. This is when submission or rejection is used as a basis for employee decisions such as promotion, retention, and so on. If the person does not agree to the sexual advances, they will not lose their job, but all the same they will not progress within the organization, or similar.
3. Harassment in the form of job interference – when such conduct has the effect of interfering with job performance or creating an intimidating, hostile or offensive working environment. This is perhaps the most obvious form of harassment when others intimidate individuals. This might take the form of lurid remarks or other offensive behaviour.

In many countries, such as the USA, the employer has liability for any sexual harassment that occurs in the workplace. However, there are many things that they can do to reduce the likelihood of sexual harassment problems.

A Look at the US Experience

The development of sexual harassment laws and policies has been very highly developed in the USA. As what happens in the USA frequently develops through the rest of the world, it is worth looking briefly at the situation there. In recent times the legislation has become more comprehensive. In particular, a ruling in the Supreme Court on 26 June 1998, made employers more liable for incidents of sexual harassment. Ruling on two sexual harassment cases, *Faragher v City of Boca Raton*, and *Burlington Industries Inc. v Ellerth*, the Supreme Court said that any employer is responsible for the actions of the supervisor, *even when the employer is unaware of the supervisor's behaviour*. Above all, an employer can no longer claim that they did not know about the sexual harassment because the employee did not inform them, nor can they claim that they were unaware of the supervisor's behaviour.

What this means is that employers must be proactive in order to avoid a sexual harassment lawsuit. So what can an employer do? The following steps are recommended:

1. Does your company have a sexual harassment policy? If not, it would make sense to get one. The usual recommendation would be that the policy should communicate that the company is taking a 'zero tolerance' approach towards sexual harassment. It is usually best to have a lawyer review it and it only has any real meaning if all of the employees in the company both have a copy and have

signed it. The policy should be verbally communicated to all new employees, and can even be posted in the workplace.

2. People are understandably wary of communicating their concerns about sexual harassment. One solution to this is to provide different routes that employees can take to file complaints. For example, you might have several different people responsible for the issue and if you are a large company you might have a phone line that employees can call to speak to someone in confidence.
3. A key point is the need to show that you are taking the issue seriously. One solution is to provide training for employees on how to deal with the problem.
4. If a dispute does arise, it is important to have a formal investigation immediately and for the whole investigation to be documented. Furthermore there should be a follow up to ensure that the problem has been resolved.
5. Advising supervisors of their duty is obviously a key area as well. They must be aware of their responsibility and regular training is recommended.

Extended Case Study: AIDS in the Workplace

In this section I want to look at the interesting area of AIDS in the workplace, primarily as an employee and employer-rights issue.

AIDS – What Is It?

AIDS is Acquired Immune Deficiency Syndrome and is caused by a virus that invades and destroys the white blood cells in the immune system. Without the immune system, the body becomes vulnerable to a range of illnesses such as pneumonia, cancer, damage to the nervous system, extreme weight loss and blindness. It is worth noting that nobody actually dies of AIDS, they die of the things that their body has no defence against. Even quite minor ailments may be sufficient. AIDS is caused by the infection of the Human Immunodeficiency Virus or HIV, as it is commonly known.

Once exposed to the HIV virus there is an incubation period of three months to ten years when they can transmit it but have no symptoms. This period is known as being HIV positive. An HIV positive person may appear perfectly healthy. That said, the disease is progressive in nature and sufferers tend to become more vulnerable to disease as time passes.

A key factor about AIDS from an ethical point of view is that the means of transmitting the disease are really quite limited. Generally, transmission is through sexual contact, exposure to infected blood and transmission between the mother and child. It can be spread through contact with blood, semen, vaginal fluids and breast milk.

It used to be thought that it was who you are that determined whether or not you got AIDS or not. Today, the view is rather different. It is what you do that really matters. The human group that you come from is not a relevant factor.

History of AIDS

There are many today who suggest that AIDS has been with us for many years. There are also many theories about how it started – from a view that it developed in monkeys through to the conspiracy theory that AIDS was the result of a biological warfare experiment. What is clear is that the first official descriptions of AIDS appeared in medical journals in 1977. However, at this time it was described as being a disease similar to pneumonia, that seemed to primarily affect homosexuals, bisexuals and people who injected drugs. It seemed to be a minority ailment and little attention was really paid to it. However, the minority disease began to spread.

In the USA, the Center for Disease Control officially diagnosed the first case of AIDS in 1981. However, even this was a very low-key affair, more of interest to the medical profession and researchers than to the mainstream public.

The death of the film actor Rock Hudson in 1985 is usually put forward as being the event that finally brought the consequences of AIDS home to the world's public. All of a sudden it became recognized that AIDS was a threat – and not just to homosexuals but to heterosexual people too. It is generally believed that by the time of Rock Hudson's death, 12,000 people in the USA were dead or dying of AIDS. By 1988 the World Health Organization had recorded 96,000 cases world-wide – although with hindsight, it is now thought that the figure was nearer 200,0000.

In 1988, a conference was held in Stockholm to assess the development of the AIDS outbreak. The conclusions are now well known and were as follows:

1. The whole world is affected. There are no countries that are AIDS-free. (It should be said that at the time of writing there were many countries that denied that they had a problem at all.)
2. There is no vaccine available. Later on in this chapter I will suggest that there may never be a vaccine.
3. No treatment or cure is really effective. Once you were infected, death was inevitable. It was just a case of how long you survived.
4. The disease has spread across all groups. The idea of it being a

homosexual disease or drug-taking disease was untenable. Anybody could get the disease, and did.

Testing for AIDS

AIDS testing revolves around testing for the antibodies that appear in the blood once someone has become infected. However, all it shows is whether you have been exposed to the virus, not that the person will conclusively get the disease or even is contagious. Perhaps more of a concern is the fact that the test is not foolproof. You can have an AIDS test show negative and still be infected. This is because it takes some time for the antibodies to build up to the point where they show up. Generally, antibodies are detectable six to twelve weeks after the infection with HIV. What this means of course is that whilst a positive test can tell you that the person does have HIV a negative test cannot prove that the person does not have HIV. However, as we will see, the implications of this may not be that serious from the workplace point of view.

What Does AIDS Mean from the Manager's Perspective?

Whichever way you look at it, nobody is immune from the effects of AIDS and the disease poses a number of questions for the business community. In particular:

- How do you handle employees with AIDS? Should you treat them differently? What happens if they become seriously ill?
- How do you educate and ensure the safety and morale of your employees? As we have seen, actually contracting AIDS is not that easy. The disease is not contagious like a cold and cannot be caught through casual contact. Most certainly it cannot be caught through hugging, sharing an office or office equipment, or sharing utensils in the company restaurant. However, there is still considerable concern amongst workers about the 'dangers' of an AIDS infected person. Even though they may accept that the AIDS carrier is not really a threat to them, they may not really be happy about working with them.
- How do you balance the needs of business with the human ethical considerations raised by the disease? This is really a stakeholder issue. You are looking to balance the rights of the individual employee with the rights of other stakeholders such as fellow workers, customers and suppliers.

Whatever the answers to these questions, AIDS is a major concern for us all. In the USA, despite the substantial improvements in medical care, the disease is still the second largest cause of death for those workers in the age bracket 25 to 44. The Center for Disease Control estimates that two thirds of companies with 2500 or more employees and nearly half the small businesses with fewer than 500 employees have had an employee with HIV or AIDS. Research has shown that despite the popular image of AIDS sufferers being drug addicts or at the margin of our society, the most likely people to be infected are most likely to be employed and mainstream workers. It is also assumed that the vast majority of people with AIDS are men. The number of women infected is increasing – and women are a very important and increasing section of the workplace.

One aspect that is rarely discussed, but should be, is the true cost of AIDS/HIV. It is well known that absence and sickness are major costs to industry. The cost of AIDS certainly may include this but there may be other costs as well, such as the cost of training and replacing people who have the misfortune to get AIDS and get sick. It is hard to measure the cost of losing individuals who die of AIDS. Another cost factor is the legal one. Particularly in the USA, AIDS has become a major legal issue and has generated more legal cases than any other disease in history.

Whatever the background, AIDS is essentially a human-rights issue.

A range of rights is involved. These might include the right to work without discrimination, the right to be treated as an equal human being, and so on. However, we might also note that a key concern for the employer is that of public health. There is an obligation on the employer to protect the health of their employees from disease and other hazards. The basic problem is as follows: on the one hand we must protect the welfare of AIDS sufferers; on the other, we need to protect the welfare of those who do not have AIDS.

A couple of key questions have to be answered:

1. Is AIDS contagious? As we have noted above, general medical opinion would say 'no'. There have been various reports about people catching AIDS from toothbrushes and so on, but most would agree that the primary methods of catching it – sexual intercourse, transfer of blood through sharing needles, blood transfusion, or mother to child, are the only really serious options. It is worth taking an opportunity to dispel a few popular myths. The following cannot cause AIDS:
   - Sharing the same room with an HIV/AIDS infected person. This will include touching or sharing the same office facilities.
   - Eating food touched by the infected person or breathing the same air as them.
   - Sharing a toilet seat with them.
   - Most light kissing.

- Transmitting the disease through mosquito bites.
- Light cuts such as paper cuts.

2. Are AIDS sufferers really handicapped employees? Should they be treated in the same way? Most countries have some legislation to deal with disabled people and having a similar strategy for AIDS sufferers would seem to make sense.

What is clear is that AIDS is not transmitted like colds or flu – it is not airborne and cannot be transmitted from coming into contact with cups or spoons used by an AIDS victim. We might also add that not everybody seems to get full-blown AIDS – even ten years after being infected half of the HIV positive people will not develop AIDS. This is a significant factor because it means that many people who are HIV positive may well be able to carry on with their lives way into the future and contribute meaningfully to society. As we will see, new medicines are giving HIV sufferers a better hope of survival.

The US Experience

In the USA since 1987 AIDS sufferers have generally been treated under the same legislation that protects handicapped people. The laws have the following implications:

- A sufferer of AIDS may be dismissed only when the condition substantially affects their ability to do their job. These are the same criteria used for disabled people. Essentially the objective is a level playing field. If someone can't do a job then the employer has the right to get rid of him or her, but they most certainly cannot get rid of someone because they have AIDS.
- There is no compulsion to hire people with AIDS, no positive discrimination – but as we have noted, an employer cannot refuse to employ someone because they have AIDS. Employees must simply be able to do their job.
- The employer must make reasonable accommodations for handicapped workers and this applies to people with AIDS. This might include letting them work flexible hours, move from full to part-time work or a less taxing position if they begin to get sick, and so on. They might also be allowed to take longer over a job than normal. The word 'reasonable' is always a difficult one and one that can often result in legal disputes. After all, what is reasonable? Courts will tend to take a wide range of factors into account. These will include the size of the business, the status of the job, and the financial state of the business. The track record of the employee may also be a factor.

- As AIDS is not contagious, employers are not expected to screen for AIDS through blood tests. However, as with for other employees, employers can test for AIDS as part of a pre-employment medical. However, if they find out that the person is HIV positive, they cannot use this as a reason for not hiring them. Neither can it be a reason to fire them if they are already in the job.

This legislation was later developed in the form of the Americans with Disabilities Act of 1990 (known as the ADA). This Act finally became effective in July 1992. The implication of this legislation was that companies with more than 25 employees that discriminated against HIV or AIDS affected workers are now liable to prosecution. What is more, the new Act has a section about people 'perceived or regarded as having HIV' because they are seen as being in a high-risk group. This might include gay men, for example. The implication would be that you could not discriminate against a member of a high-risk group on the grounds that they 'are the sort of person who might get AIDS'.

The main conclusions of the ADA are as follows:

1. Disabled persons should receive the same employment opportunities as anyone else.
2. Employers must clearly justify the use of any employee standard, criterion or job description that tends to exclude or adversely affect disabled workers.

As we have noted, the biggest problem with AIDS/HIV is not the real threat that it poses but the perceived threat. What happens if you have an AIDS-infected worker, and this frightens customers off? Despite all of the education and publicity, a large number of people in the USA and Europe still have very negative and discriminatory views of people with HIV and AIDS. Some employers too, it should be said, have tended to ignore HIV as a workplace concern because they prefer to deny it exists.

Another issue put forward by some is the potentially reduced working life of someone with AIDS/HIV. This is probably a red herring. Other people may well have the same potential problem. We might include people with heart conditions or people who smoke or people who have a family history of cancer. Are we going to discriminate against them as well? In addition, we might note that these days people are less likely to spend a long time in a single job anyway. Furthermore, the life expectancy of people with AIDS/HIV has tended to increase as medical science has improved.

Organizations have tried to come up with various solutions to the AIDS/HIV problem. One solution that some firms are applying is to continue to pay people with AIDS on full salary and medical benefits but not actually give them any work – even give them pay rises. Essentially they are paying them to stay at home. If the person is happy about this, you might suggest that this is a good solution. Personally I would suggest that this is not a satisfactory solution. In a sense you are removing a basic human right, the right to work. There is also evidence that people who work are more likely to live longer and better. The sudden decline of people who retire is a case in point. Take away the reason for living and people die. The same could apply to an AIDS victim.

Have an AIDS Policy

Many organizations have an AIDS policy and this can certainly be recommended. What should it contain? Most organizations work on the following basis:

- The policy is based on the recognition that HIV/AIDS is not contagious. Therefore people with the disease do not have to be screened off or given special working conditions.
- All human beings gain self-identity and self-esteem from work. Therefore keeping people at work is the ideal scenario. As we have noted, working at your regular job often enhances good health. Therefore all workers should be allowed to determine for themselves how long they are able to carry on rather being forced to stay at home or whatever.
- All companies have an obligation to provide a safe working place for their employees and customers. This is the public health issue that we have noted. However, AIDS does not usually prevent a public health threat in a normal working environment such as in an office.
- AIDS cannot be cured but it can be stopped. Education and information are the key to handling AIDS in a satisfactory manner.
- We have to recognize the rights of all stakeholders in the business. The treatment of AIDS-infected individuals must recognize this. The objective is to be fair to all concerned. We shall look at the concept of stakeholders in more depth in Chapter 6. Essentially, a stakeholder is anyone who does have an interest (stake) in the business. In this case, they might include other employees, customers, suppliers and the local environment.
- Confidentiality is important. We would never publicize a person's medical records, so we should not publicize the fact that someone has AIDS/HIV. They have a right to confidentiality if they wish it.

- Any person refusing to work with an AIDS-infected worker will be counselled. In extreme cases, they may be warned and be subject to dismissal. However, every step should be taken to avoid this.
- A key objective should be to encourage workers through training and counselling to support those with HIV/AIDS.

A Sample AIDS Policy

The US organization SHRM have produced a sample AIDS policy, which is released into the public domain on the World Wide Web and is available for use or modification by any organization that wishes to. It is an excellent policy draft and I am attaching a copy below.

The following is a sample policy for you to use as a guide when creating a statement for your organization. The policy is an important first step. It sets the tone for communicating about HIV as a workplace and productivity issue. Policy statements should be educational in tone and provide guidance for employees in terms of procedures and resources. You can adapt this statement or use sections of it as you see fit.

(Company) does not unlawfully discriminate against employees or applicants living with or affected by HIV (Human Immunodeficiency Virus) or AIDS (Acquired Immune Deficiency Syndrome). The (Company) recognizes that HIV infection and AIDS, the most serious stage of disease progression resulting from HIV infection, pose significant and delicate issues for the workplace. Accordingly, we have established the following guidelines and principles to serve as the basis for handling employee situations and concerns related to HIV infection and AIDS.

I

The (Company) is committed to maintaining a safe and healthy work environment for all employees. This commitment stands on the recognition that HIV, and therefore AIDS, is not transmitted through any casual contact.

HIV is a blood borne virus and is spread only through intimate contact with blood, semen, vaginal secretions, and breast milk. For over ten years, scientists have made new discoveries about HIV infection and AIDS. But one piece of information has never changed – how the disease spreads. Scientists have recognized this fact since 1982. The basic facts about HIV transmission and prevention are sound.

II

The (Company) will treat HIV infection and AIDS the same as other illnesses in terms of all of our employee policies and benefits, including health and life insurance, disability benefits and leaves of absence. Employees living with or affected by HIV infection and AIDS will be treated with compassion and understanding, as would employees with other disabling conditions.

III

In accordance with the law, the (Company) will provide reasonable accommodations for employees and applicants with disabilities who are qualified to perform the essential functions of their positions. This applies to employees and applicants living with HIV infection and AIDS, and is especially relevant in light of new treatments for HIV infection that may allow people living with AIDS to return to work after periods of disability leave.

Generally, disabled employees have the responsibility to request an accommodation. It is the policy of (the Company) to respond to the changing health status of employees by making reasonable accommodations. Employees may continue to work as long as they are able to perform their duties safely and in accordance with performance standards. Supervisors and managers are encouraged to contact the Human Resources Department for assistance in making reasonable accommodations.

IV

Co-worker concerns will be handled in an educational fashion. The Human Resources Department can provide information and educational materials. In addition, the names of community-based organizations in our operating areas are appended. Consult one of these groups for support and information. Supervisors and managers are encouraged to contact the Human Resources Department for assistance in providing employees with information and assistance.

Recognizing the need for all employees to be accurately informed about HIV infection and AIDS, the (Company) will make information and educational materials and seminars available. Employees who want to obtain information and materials should contact the Human Resources Department.

V

Co-workers are expected to continue working relationships with any employee who has HIV infection or AIDS. Co-workers, who refuse to work with, withhold services from, harass or otherwise discriminate against an employee with HIV infection or AIDS will be subject to the same disciplinary procedures that apply to other policy violations.

VI

Information about an employee's medical condition is private and must be treated in a confidential manner. In most cases, only mangers directly involved in providing a reasonable accommodation or arranging benefits may need to know an employee's diagnosis. Others who may acquire such information, even if obtained personally from the individual, should respect the confidentiality of the medical information.

VII

(Company) maintains an 'open-door' policy. Employees living with or affected by HIV infection and AIDS, and those who have any related concerns, are encouraged to contact their supervisor, office administrator, their department director, the Employee Relations and Development Manager, or the Chief Administrative Officer to discuss their concerns and obtain information.

If you have questions about this policy, its interpretation, or the information upon which it is based, please contact any of the individuals listed in item #7 above.

Appendix: List of local HIV/AIDS information and service organizations (optional).

There is considerable evidence that putting AIDS policies into place and ensuring that there are AIDS educational policies in the company before it becomes a problem can be very effective in dealing with any case that does come along. One big advantages is that having these policies tends to break down prejudice and helps create a better, more supportive environment for the HIV/AIDS infected worker. There is also ample evidence that workers would like to have AIDS/HIV training.

The AIDS/HIV problem may extend beyond the workplace, of course. The family of the AIDS/HIV worker will need support. They may well feel discriminated against and certainly frustration will be a problem. SHRM have also provided the following list of recommendations for an AIDS/HIV programme which is also worthy of note:

Steps for Planning Your HIV/AIDS Education Program

- Approach management with this issue as a business issue and take the steps necessary to get support from your chief executive officer and senior management. (See the Business Case section for information about HIV as a business issue.)

- Compile information on HIV/AIDS and on what other organizations similar to yours have done.
- Identify a leader who can champion the cause for an HIV/AIDS Education Program. If there is more than one person who is well suited for the opportunity, then develop a team.
- Encourage teamwork.
- Educate yourself on this issue so that you can educate others.
- Define your company's position on this issue by developing an *HIV/AIDS workplace policy*.
- Gather information about resources and use them as needed. There are a number of excellent providers of HIV education programs for workplaces. See the *Resources Section* for referrals and linkages to resources available to you.
- Plan your budget; including the cost of materials (brochures, videos, flyers, reprints, etc.), a speaker(s) who is an expert in the field, your time and the time of team members, and meeting room costs (if any).

Steps for Planning Your HIV/AIDS Education Activities

- Plan to train Managers and Supervisors so that they are knowledgeable about HIV/AIDS.
- Develop a marketing communications plan so that you send the message that you intend to send and communicate the basic information needed to avoid potential confusion around the issue and your efforts. Try to allow for opportunities where there can be open communication.
- Plan to hold employee meetings (in small groups) to explain your organization's HIV/AIDS workplace policy, information on how HIV/AIDS is transmitted, prevention methods, company benefits available to employees afflicted with the disease, confidentiality requirements, etc.

Bear in mind that a workplace HIV/AIDS Training Program should communicate to employers the following:

- How HIV is transmitted.
- How HIV is NOT transmitted.
- Why it is okay for someone with HIV to be in the workplace.
- The importance of implementing universal precautions in all first-aid situations.
- The importance of keeping all medical information confidential.
- Where to turn in the workplace and in the community for information and resources.

> After getting support from the top, implement the program by holding the employee meetings. Request that your chief executive officer or another company official introduce the program, and encourage employee discussion and questions. The most effective educational/training programs are those where the information is presented clearly and consistently.
>
> Most organizations have found that implementing such a program is beneficial to both the employer and employees. Because there is no cure to date for HIV/AIDS, developing and implementing a sound program does, in fact, make good business sense.

What can be agreed is that the provision of an AIDS policy can make a great deal of difference to the working of an organization. Above all else, managing AIDS/HIV is all about *education.*

The Two Worlds of AIDS

So far we have spoken primarily about the USA and other parts of the developed world. One factor that is becoming increasingly clear is that the AIDS problem is splitting into two very separate worlds. On the one hand there is the situation in wealthy countries of the world – such as in the USA, Northern Europe and parts of the Far East – and then there is the very different picture presented in the developing world.

On the face of it, the picture in the developed world is improving all of the time. Recent research in the USA has produced a cocktail of drugs that can put the disease in remission. As a result, some insurance companies have started to offer life insurance to AIDS sufferers. Research has also shown that there are now two rare genetic variations that seem to give AIDS patients immunity. In addition to this, treatments are now available that greatly prolong life, particularly if the treatment is started before symptoms start when the immune system is still strong.

However, good although this news is, there is a catch. The current cost of treatment is very high. The cocktail of drugs, for example costs around £20,000 per annum so it is actually of very little value to the majority of AIDS sufferers. Around 90 per cent of those with AIDS in the world are from the developing world.

A United Nations study in 1997 reported that 30.6 million people worldwide had the AIDS virus. It is now believed that now we have reached the year 2000, the figure is around 40 million, although opinion differs on this. It is believed that around 19 million people have died from it. The quality of information on this subject is not always reliable. What is clear is the huge disparity between the wealthy and poor parts of the word. In sub-Saharan Africa, 7.4 per cent of adults (or around 20.8

million people) are infected, as compared to 0.6 per cent of adults in North America.

The key issue with AIDS is that it means different things to different people. The expensive new treatments that we mentioned have made the suffering of AIDS in the wealthy parts of the world far less onerous. In the USA deaths due to AIDS fell by around 30 per cent per annum during the late 1990s. AIDS is now regarded as an annoying, though ultimately deadly, infection in wealthier areas of the world.

This is a massive contrast with Sub-Saharan Africa. AIDS is a major concern in parts of Latin America and many parts of Asia but Sub-Saharan Africa is certainly the largest area of concern. Peter Piot, head of UNAIDS, estimates that 7.4 per cent of Africans in the age group 15 to 49 are infected. The trouble is that in Africa, voluntary testing is really quite rare so at least 90 per cent of these people don't know that they are infected. As we have noted, the figure can only be an estimate as well because of the poor levels of information generated in these countries.

Some countries are worse than others. Uganda and Botswana are generally reckoned to be the countries with the biggest problem. In Uganda, the average life expectancy has actually fallen from 53.2 to 40.3 years since the early 1980s. Up to 0.5 million Ugandan people have died from AIDS and 1.6 million are infected – around 12 per cent of the country's population.

Infection rates in Uganda are just starting to come down. However, this is owing to saturation of the disease. Basically people are dying from AIDS quicker than people are being infected. Uganda is rare in that it has acknowledged that it has a crisis.

In Botswana it is believed that the rate of infection is around 36 per cent of adults. Even wealthier South Africa, it might be noted, has a rate of around 20 per cent. Many African countries are not admitting to the problem because of the threat to tourism. Interestingly, in the West, AIDS started as a homosexual disease but became a heterosexual one. In Africa, it has always been a heterosexual one.

What is the Solution?

Given the very high cost of the drugs, the most likely person in the world to take them is a homosexual man from a rich Western country – USA, Europe, Australia or New Zealand. We might note that the cost of these drugs can run up to several hundred thousand pounds from the time of diagnosis of the disease to the time of death. In contrast, hospitals in some parts of Africa, where annual health care spend per person may be less than $10 per person, may lack basic drugs like aspirin. Elizabeth Marun, the AIDS coordinator for the US Agency for International Development in Uganda, suggests, 'Researches like to say that if a cure for Aids were a single glass of clean water, most of the HIV positive people in Africa would still be doomed.'

Will There Ever Be a Vaccine?

It is the view of many, and certainly this writer, that it is very unlikely that there will ever be a vaccine for AIDS. On the face of it, this seems a startling conclusion, but there is a strong foundation behind this view.

The main problem seems to be that the drug companies have little incentive to develop one. The level of medical research aimed at AIDS is really quite limited. Only a tenth of the 1.5 billion AIDS research budget at the National Institute of Health is aimed at vaccines and drug companies are believed to devote only $20 million per year on vaccine development, which is a tiny amount on a relative scale. Why is this? As with most things the reason seems to be money. In the USA, people can afford to keep themselves alive with life-enhancing drugs, but the main sufferers on the planet are in the developing world and they have no money at all. Why should a drugs company develop drugs for people who could not afford them? What is more, their governments cannot afford them either.

Remember that we asked, at the start of the book, if capitalism is just? It is an interesting thought that we live in a world where we will produce Viagra, a drug that enhances male sexuality at high cost, but we will not produce a drug to save the lives of millions.

The conclusion seems to be this. For the vast majority of people in the world, it is education rather than drugs that is going to save them. And not just in the developing world. At the time of writing it was noted that there were an increasing number of young homosexual men taking risks by having unprotected sex and frequent partners. In another report, the Public Health Laboratory Service released new figures that the number of people in the UK with HIV was actually rising at a rate of around 10,000 per year and that the rate of infection among people aged 15 to 49 was around one in 1000. Although the problem in developed countries may be nothing in comparison with those in Africa, for example, it is clearly all too easy for us to become complacent.

What do we do about AIDS at work? I think that we can conclude that the best solution to the problem is understanding and tolerance through education. However, it is by no means a straightforward issue. Consider the following classic case by Robert Taylor, and ask yourself how you would deal with this situation – which is based on a true story.

CASE STUDY – **AIDS in the Workplace** (*by Robert Taylor*)

Your firm of attorneys acts as the legal counsel to David Barry, the owner and general manager of the Cork and Cleaver Restaurant, a bar/restaurant catering for young professional people in a mid-sized eastern city. David has come into your office for advice. His MBA degree from a local university hardly prepared him to confront the ethical dilemma he now faces. This morning, the former wife of one of his employees had come to him with confidential information about Tom Johnson, the twenty-four-year-old cook that he had hired only five months ago. Tom, she told him, has AIDS. David advised you that Tom, although new on the job, have been an above-average employee in the restaurant. He was still in his probationary period of employment however, and could be terminated without cause. After his six-month evaluation, based on his good record so far, Tom could expect to receive permanent employment together with a pensions and benefit plan, and be subject to termination only for a valid reason.

In attempting to decide what action if any should be taken, David asks you the following questions:

- How do you think that news of the disease might affect the thirteen colleagues of Tom, some of whom had been close friends?
- How might the news affect customers and business?

You have been tasked to produce the ideas for a letter to David outlining the legal, economic and moral issues that faces him as owner of the Cork and Cleaver.

Pause for thought . . .
How should you deal with the situation in the case study? I would suggest to you that the key is in comparing the rights of all the stakeholders involved. You might well find going back to Green's excellent NORM approach useful here as well. How might Kant's 'universal rule' be applied here as well?

Conclusion

The issue of worker rights is a very difficult one. The main problem, as we have seen from the many examples discussed, is that there is often a clear conflict between the rights of the individual in society and the rights of the employee in the workplace. Very often, individual rights are sacrificed on the altar of workplace rules. Governments can certainly put in place extensive legislation, but in the end it is really down to the individual employer to manage this difficult problem.

CHAPTER 5

The Ethics of Marketing Communications

Promotion Techniques

One of the main developments in the field of marketing communications has been the tightening up of the claims that promoters can make. Even claims that were made in the 1960s are no longer acceptable. For example, two claims made in the 1960s that became well known were:

'Guinness is good for you'
and
'Persil washes whiter'

Neither of these would be acceptable in the UK today, although they are still used in some countries. On the face of it, the claims are fairly harmless, but they do have their difficulties. The claim of 'Guinness is good for you' may be right up to a point, but equally, the consumption of very large amounts may be very bad for you indeed. With the Persil claim, white is clearly an absolute and you cannot have 'whiter'. In addition, the claim is almost impossible to substantiate. What does 'whiter' really mean anyway?

However, these claims were relatively innocent compared with some of the advertising used 100 years ago. Perhaps the most famous example was that of the Carbolic Smoke Ball Company whose advertising claim was that their product:

1. Cured coughs in one week.
2. Cured all colds within twelve hours.
3. Relieved whooping cough.
4. Cured bronchitis and around a dozen other ailments.

It is worth noting what a carbolic smoke ball is. Essentially it is an incense burner that burns carbolic soap to give off a vapour, which acted as a decongestant. As you will imagine, acting as a decongestant was a far cry from curing the above ailments, many of which were major killers. The company made a further claim with the advertisement. They said that they would pay out £100 to anybody who caught influenza after using the Carbolic Smoke Ball. In the event, a lady did catch flu and made a claim. The company answered that the claim was after all only an advert and they could not realistically be expected to honour a claim like that. In the event, the matter went to court and in a landmark ruling they were forced to pay up.

Other advertisers were more subtle. Take for example Bovril who featured a picture of the Pope drinking Bovril and wrote that it was a picture of 'two infallible powers'.

Gradually, things were tightened up through both legislation and self-regulation and today advertising in particular is far more rigorously controlled. For example:

1. *Alcohol and cigarettes* Tobacco and alcohol advertising have both proved to be very popular targets for control, primarily because of the potential of both to cause ill health and death. In addition, both have been the subjects of much pressure from activist groups who have lobbied the control authorities around the world. The primary argument against advertising these products is that it increases the consumption of them. Given that they are potentially or actually harmful, this is not deemed desirable. The manufacturers of the products and others have suggested that although it would seem to be the case, there is no real evidence that the advertisements actually increase consumption. The manufacturers argue that all the advertising is doing is taking brand share from one brand and giving it to another.
2. *Advertising aimed at children* – In many countries, advertising aimed at children is banned. Since the 1970s, there has been an increasing concern about the effects of advertising on children. A key factor in advertising is the idea of the 'influence and yield effect'. This suggests that children will have a big impact on what their parents buy, not just for products that they might have a direct interest in, but all sorts of items. The washing machine

manufacturer Whirlpool once ran a campaign aimed at a youth audience, targeting them with a view to getting them to persuade their parents to buy a Whirlpool washing machine. From a marketing point of view, this is a strong strategy, but the ethics of it are perhaps a little unclear. Children may well be very brand aware (children as young as 4 seem to have some brand awareness), but their ability to make rational choices may not be as strong. Is this therefore acceptable?

Of course the biggest issue in this area is the question of adverts actually targeted at children – the Saturday morning toy advert, for example, where the child is encouraged to nag their parents into buying the product. Again, some countries feel that this strategy is immoral and that it exploits immature minds.

It might be noted that there are no such controls in the USA or UK, even though there have been numerous attempts to change the rules. A key factor, which we will keep coming back to, is this: it is all very well saying that we should ban things, but what about the rights of the manufacturers to advertise their wares? How else are they going to promote their products?

Norway and several other countries have banned several forms of sales promotion such as trading stamps, competitions and premiums as being inappropriate or unfair for promoting products. This might seem a very strange action, but it has a strong reason supporting it. The thinking is that very often the product is bought not because of the product itself but because of the premium attached to it. The promotion becomes the reason for purchase. Let me give you an example. Imagine that you have a young child and are buying breakfast cereal. In each of the cereal packets there is a free plastic dinosaur. The child has collected most of them but the red one is still proving elusive. What do you do? You could end up buying loads of packets in the hope that you find the red one! The same applies to offers that require so many packet tops by a certain time. If you don't consume the product quickly enough, you end up buying more than you can get through. What are you buying here, the product or the promotion? For this reason, some countries do control or limit sales promotion.

A number of developing countries put stronger controls on promotion. For example, Thailand has required food manufacturers selling national brands to market low-price goods as well so that low-income consumers can find low-price brands on the shelves. In India, food companies need special approval to launch brands that duplicate what already exists on the market, such as another cola drink or another rice.

Privacy

More recently a number of other areas have become important. Privacy is an interesting question. Traditionally, mass-market communication has not made many inroads into privacy. However, the growth of direct marketing and now the Internet has begun to change things. There are many rules set up to protect the privacy of individuals from overzealous direct marketing and it appears that these may have to be extended to the Internet.

The UK Example

This textbook is being written in the UK, so it would seem appropriate to look at the UK's approach to advertising control. In the UK, TV advertising is restricted to only six minutes per hour for terrestrial TV and many things are banned:

- cigarettes
- political organizations
- religious bodies
- dating agencies
- betting shops

It has to be said that at the time of writing there are some moves afoot to change this situation. The betting industry in particular has opposed controls on the grounds that the National Lottery is allowed to advertise. The betting industry has reasonably argued that there is no difference between the two.

Controls in the UK

The situation in the UK is complicated when it comes to controls. The Advertising Standards Authority (ASA) regulates most media. However, television is under much greater control. The body responsible for television is the Independent Broadcasting Authority and this has a strict code of advertising practice with special sections on children, finances and medicines. Most importantly, all advertisements have to be vetted before televising. This tends to overcome the problems associated with corrective advertising, an issue that we will discuss later on in the chapter. How acceptable are controls like this?

The code of the ASA in the UK is shown below as a good example of the sort of thinking applied to advertising controls:

- Adverts should contain nothing that is likely to cause serious widespread offence.

- Care should be taken with race, religion, sex, sexual orientation or disability.
- Compliance will be judged on the context, medium, audience, product and prevailing standards of decency.
- Adverts may be distasteful without necessarily conflicting with the above.
- Advertisers are urged to consider public sensitivities before using potentially offensive material.
- The fact that a product is offensive to some people is not sufficient grounds for objecting to the advert for it.

The Value of Advertising

There are many who would argue that advertising should be cut down considerably. A variety of arguments have been put for and against the morality of advertising and it is worthwhile looking at these. They are as follows:

1. Advertising is just a waste of money. Huge amounts of money are spent on advertising that could be spent on more worthwhile projects such as hospitals and schools. The industry employs lots of talented people who could be gainfully employed in more socially acceptable jobs.
2. Advertising encourages wasteful consumption: it encourages people to buy things that they don't really need. Essentially the charge is that advertising manipulates us – changes our behaviour in a way that suits the advertiser.
3. The very high costs of advertising prevent new companies coming into the market. This is known as a barrier to entry. Many fast-moving consumer goods companies' expenditure is so high that they gain a lot of power in an industry, and power creates margins. The example of the soap-powder industry, that is dominated by two companies, Proctor & Gamble and Unilever, is often cited. These two companies are both huge spenders on advertising and yet the activity appears to be directed at gaining very small changes in market share.
4. Advertising deceives those who are unable to judge the truth of advertising claims. We have already mentioned the question of advertising to children. Children are a good example because they are certainly brand aware but perhaps lack the discretion to really know about realistic choices. Having said that, such allegations are difficult to prove. In truth in the short term it may be possible to deceive people but the real measure of success is the repeat pur-

chase. You might be able to deceive people once, but a deceived customer is not likely to come back for more.

5. Advertising sometimes exploits women. This may not be as much of a problem as it was and, in fact, there is actually quite a lot of evidence that sex only works well as an advertising medium if it is related to the subject. Recall tests on men in particular show that people don't remember the goods but remember the model so its use as a marketing tool is questionable.
6. Advertising uses shock tactics too often. In many countries, the use of these tactics has to be justified and for this reason they are most often used in government advertising (campaigns against drink driving, for example). However, a range of other organizations have also used shock tactics, and the ethics of this have been called into question. Some examples are given below.

CASE STUDY – **The Breast Cancer Fund**

In the USA, the Breast Cancer Fund caused considerable outrage with a campaign showing models with mastectomy scars. In one ad, a cover girl coyly pulls down her bra to show a deep scar instead of a breast. The scars belong to the charity's founder, Andrea Martin, and have been superimposed on models – but critics claim the message could backfire and deter women from seeking medical help. The question of taste is also clear here. Certainly, breast cancer is a major issue and awareness of it should be improved. But is this the best way to do it?

CASE STUDY – **Benetton**

Benetton has become famous for its controversial advertising. There have been many examples of this. Perhaps the most famous is entitled *Looking at death in the face*. This is a study of prisoners on death row. One inmate is reading a Bible and all are looking straight at the camera claiming that, despite everything, they should have rights as human beings.

Benetton defended the advertisement, saying that it aimed at giving back a human face to the prisoners and to challenge the views of respectable people about the issue. This might be the case, although advertising strategy theory does suggest that the best way of advertising something unremarkable – such as a range of colourful knitwear – is to use advertising that is nothing to do with the actual product. The real motives of Benetton have never really been clear and have always been a source of considerable controversy.

CASE STUDY – **Barnardo's**

Giving children back their future is a warning that drug addiction can be related to childhood. It shows a baby using his gums to clench a tourniquet around his chubby arm with a syringe in his hand. The image was created with the help of computer graphics.

The editorial reads: 'battered as a child, it was always possible John would turn to drugs. With Barnardo's help, child abuse need not lead to an empty future.' This was the final image of a hard-hitting campaign, which also showed children as homeless, suicidal, alcoholics and jailbirds. Claire Hall, media officer for Barnardo's, says the aim was not to shock but to use a powerful image to highlight a serious issue, 'We wanted to get people's attention as part of our effort to help children.'

Analysis

The real question with advertising like this has to be the motivation behind it and also the effect of it. Is the advertising trying to make people think about an issue, or to draw their attention to an otherwise rather mundane product? Even if it does draw attention to an important social issue, can we justify the upset that it might cause? In the event the UK ASA said that it received 25 complaints about the Benetton advertisement when it was published and 19 for the Barnardo's. This is a relatively small number considering the interest the advertisements have generated. A cynic might suggest that most people would not know how to complain or would not bother to complain because it wouldn't have any effect. The ASA counters this by saying that in fact its simple to complain – one letter is enough. On receipt of the letter, the ASA will then consider whether the advert has broken its guidelines. What is acceptable is not always clear cut.

A range of factors may have to be taken into account. The location of the advert may be relevant. What might be acceptable in the pages of a male magazine may not be deemed suitable for a hoarding in the town centre. If the ASA considers the advert has caused serious offence, it will ask the advertiser to withdraw it. If they refuse, the media is advised not to accept it.

There can be no doubt that advertising does have its detractors. People who work in advertising are often aware that the public has a low opinion of them. A good example of this is that when the prominent advertising man Jacques Seguela wrote a book, he called it *Don't tell my mother I'm in advertising – She thinks I'm a pianist in a brothel.* However, there is evidence to suggest that many of the criticisms that we have discussed are not justified. Let us consider some of the positive aspects of advertising:

1. There is much evidence that advertising in recessions does keep the business going. The logic behind this is straightforward. Recessions are generally caused by a lack of confidence amongst the population. Consumers do not buy because they are afraid of losing their jobs. Of course, this very action threatens jobs because people not buying means people not working. Something has to break this cycle. It can be argued that advertising can reduce the effects of recession because it can encourage people to buy things they are not quite sure about.
2. Rather than increasing prices by adding to costs, advertising increases consumption and volume and therefore actually benefits everybody. It can be argued that much of the improvements that have occurred in the past hundred years or so in human consumption have been because of increased volume and economies of scale. People buy more which reduces the cost of production so people buy more and on it goes. Advertising, it can be argued, increases sales and therefore reduces costs. This cost reduction pays for the advertising. Therefore advertising is free!
3. There is a lot of evidence to suggest that people actually enjoy advertising and that often the commercials are preferred to the programmes although others find them annoying. I am sure that we all have our favourite advertisement. You could well argue that advertising is an art form with an artistic value all of its own. Why should it be stopped?
4. Advertising has been a proving ground for many film directors, photographers and artists. Along with pop videos, advertising certainly provides many opportunities for new directors and other artists that might not be available otherwise. Of course, as we have already mentioned, advertising is a major industry that gives employment to many thousands of people.
5. Advertising can also be used for much socially correct work such as religions or charities. Advertising is a communication tool and therefore, it can be argued, there is nothing wrong with it in itself.

If it is abused, that is a different matter. Advertising can certainly be used for good causes.

Advertising Controls in the USA

The primary argument, particularly in the USA, has always been that the control of advertising is a breach of freedom of speech – essentially a breach of First Amendment rights. The First Amendment places controls on the government's ability to repress speech. How does this influence advertising? Well, advertising is regarded within the Constitution as a form of 'commercial speech'. Commercial speech is that which 'does no more than propose a commercial action'. Essentially something that makes someone buy something. So is 'commercial speech' – or advertising – something that can be government regulated? The answer is yes, but only under certain conditions. These are:

1. If the advert is misleading or concerns an illegal product.
2. If there is substantial government interest.
3. If the regulation directly advances that government interest.
4. If the regulation is narrowly tailored to that interest.

In simple terms the government can regulate, but only in very limited circumstances. Any other controls are put under the auspices of the Federal Trade Commission (FTC) – we will discuss this body shortly. Should there be any regulation anyway? Many businesses argue that the cost of regulation can actually be higher than the benefits. Complaints that are put forward include:

1. The laws are not always administered fairly.
2. The laws may hurt many legitimate firms and prevent legitimate entry. In other words, the restrictions may prevent entry barriers in an industry.

The USA accounts for around 50 per cent of the world's advertising spend and for this reason it is worth looking at the controlling body for this vast market.

The FTC is an independent law-enforcement agency charged by Congress with the regulation of deceptive advertising. It was formed as a result of the FTC Act of 1914. Section 5 of the Act gave the Commission the authority to regulate 'unfair methods of competition'. In 1938 the Wheeler Lea Act added foods and drugs to the list to be regulated by the FTC and also changed the FTC's authority to include 'unfair or deceptive acts or practices'. It is this added power that applies to advertising. The FTC has been given progressively more power over the years. A good example of this was in 1967 when the Federal Cigarette Labelling and Advertising Act required a statutory warning on cigarettes. The FTC monitors this.

The commissioners of the FTC act like judges, hearing cases where advertisers have been accused of violating the FTC Act. Rather like the ASA in the UK, they also provide guidelines for advertisers. The FTC has the power to stop business practices that restrict competition or deceive consumers, providing that they fall within the statues of the FTC and the issue related to interstate business. The FTC has the power to stop businesses either by:

issuing 'cease and desist' orders; or
taking out legal injunctions through the Federal courts.

Equally significant, the FTC defines which practices violate the law so that business people know where they stand and the issues upon which action can be taken.

The medium the FTC uses is 'The trade regulation Rules and Industry Guide', which is basically a list of do's and don'ts. The Commission also operates an advisory service called Advisory Opinions so if anybody is not sure if they are likely to violate they can ask first.

The FTC has considerable power. In the case of isolated incidents of deceptive advertising, the FTC can make complaints and stop individual ads. In more serious cases, the FTC can impose serious fines through the Federal civil courts. In addition to this, it can also seek redress for those who have been harmed by dubious advertising, including getting people's money back, or the return of property and payments for damages.

A good example of the FTC's work is when a well-known personality is used to endorse a product. It is well known by marketing people that the use of top personalities causes extremely strong responses because of their fame and 'likeability'. They are very strong opinion leaders and can have a powerful impact on sales. This is known as the 'Q' factor in the entertainment and advertising industry. However, there are problems with the use of these people. There have been several cases where an advert has been vetoed by the FTC unless the personality concerned has particular knowledge or of some known association with the product. A particular problem has been where the same personality has been used to advertise a range of products. How can they be genuinely expected to know about all of these? In reality, these FTC controls may not be that serious. They may give problems to advertisers but also may increase creativity in the long run. In addition, there are many alternatives to advertisers using personalities to advertise products.

Deceptive Practices

Deceptive practices in the FTC have centred mainly on the more subtle abuses of advertising. Many businesses that have been accused of advertising problems have used the First Amendment in arguing against the action – basically that the freedom of speech has been damaged.

In 1976 in a case *Virginia State Board v Virginia Citizens Consumer Council* it was ruled that it was in a matter of the public interest that private economic decisions be intelligent and well informed. To this end the free flow of commercial information is indispensable.

The Court was reaffirming the First Amendment Rights of the public to know facts relevant to decision-making in the marketplace.

On the other hand, the Supreme Court held in the case of *Bates v the USA* in 1977 that this First Amendment protection of advertising was entirely dependent upon its truthfulness. 'The public and private benefits from commercial speech derives from confidence in its accuracy and reliability.' In other cases the courts have gone on to say that truthfulness in advertising includes completeness of information as well as the absence of misleading or incorrect information.

The key requirement is that the advertisers have a reasonable basis to substantiate the claim before an ad has been run. *If you are not able to substantiate the claim beforehand then it is a violation even if the ad was not deceptive.*

A key criticism of the FTC is that it was always after the fact – it could only act after the ad was put in and often simply by telling the offender not to do it again. However, more recently the FTC has actually been insisting on remedial action such as corrective advertising, which is potentially a very harsh punishment.

In the mid-1970s, the FTC ordered the Warner Lambert Co. to include a corrective message in their next $10 million of advertising. The message would have to say that Listerine was not effective against colds and sore throats contrary to their previous claims. More recently, Volvo was asked to retract when an ad involved driving a monster truck over a number of cars. In the event only the Volvo was undamaged. In reality the Volvo had been strengthened especially for the ad. The company's president was asked to write a corrective letter, explaining what had been done. Such a corrective position is only used if a long-term effect has occurred. There is also some evidence that corrective advertising can be too harsh. Consumers tend to generalize and can end up having a negative view of the brand as a whole, not just the one ad.

Another argument is that the make-up and regulation of the FTC make the organization too close to the government. During the Reagan and Bush years, the FTC eased its advertising substantiation requirements in an effort to balance both industry and consumer demands while keeping down the cost of the products. The FTC still requires substantiation of advertised claims about a product's safety performance, quality and comparative price. In recent years, however, critics have accused the FTC of pursuing only the most blatant cases and of focusing enforcement efforts on smaller advertisers – that is those advertisers who were least able to and least likely to dispute the FTC directives.

In addition to FTC oversight, deceptive advertising among major advertisers is usually limited by competitive reaction. For example, many large advertisers have sued each other because of conflicting superiority claims. In a dispute between oil companies, Castrol Inc. sued the Pennzoil company over Pennzoil's claim to 'outperform any leading motor oil against viscosity breakdown'. The Gillette company sued Wilkinson Sword Inc. for claiming that the Wilkinson sword Ultra Glide blades were superior to Gillette's Extra Plus blades.

There are signs that this self-regulation is increasing. A good example from the UK is where the self-regulatory body the Portman Group, set up by the drinks industry, passed a ruling that stopped manufacturers of alcoholic drinks using such words as 'energizing' or 'stimulating'. Although not a legal body, the Portman Group has considerable power. Those advertisers who do not desist from such claims can have complaints made against them. These complaints could result in the Portman Group advising retailers not to stock their products.

The FDA distinguishes between an unfair advert and a deceptive advert. An unfair advert is one in which the advertiser withholds information that could result in some form of injury to the consumer whereas a deceptive ad contains explicit or implied claims, which are likely to mislead a consumer. Most ads that fall foul come into three categories:

1. Where completely false claims are made.
2. Where some relevant qualifications of a claim are omitted, resulting in misrepresentation.
3. Where no deceptive claim is made explicitly but a belief is still created.

Perhaps the last is the worse because it is very hard to stop. For example, if a candy bar is described as 'wholesome' it suggests that it meets national standards for nutrients whether it does or not. Another good example occurs in food labelling where labels claim that a product has 'no preservatives, no artificial ingredients' but this obscures the fact that colouring agents may be added to enhance the product's appearance (for example, onion soup often contains caramel powder to make it look darker and richer). Another example occurred when Perrier claimed that their water was 'calorie free'. This was misleading because water does not have any calories anyway.

Conclusion

The question of managing ethics in the marketing communication field is a difficult and controversial one. Again, the issue is really one of balance. The rights of individual companies to express what they want to express about their products and services within a free-market economy have to be set against the public concerns about misleading or unsuitable advertising. The problem is particularly compounded in cases such as cigarette advertising where a legal product has very restrictive advertising controls placed upon it. Perhaps the real question is this: Have advertising controls gone too far?

CHAPTER 6

The Rights of Stakeholders

Over the next few sections of the book, I want to discuss the idea of stakeholders – who they are, and how they fit into the business ethics picture. We have already mentioned them when we spoke about the idea of Green's NORM. In simple terms, a stakeholder is any group of people who have a stake in our business. Clearly, the employees we discussed in Chapter 4 are a stakeholder group but there are many more and it would be useful to discover who they are.

A very important question to consider is this. For whose benefit should a business be run?

The law of corporations, which are similar throughout the world, make the answer to this question really very straightforward. It says that the corporation should be run in the interests of the shareholders. As a result of this, the directors have an obligation to the shareholders of the business. The directors are appointed by the shareholders and have a responsibility to maximize their wealth. Should the directors not do this then they run the risk of being voted off the board.

Central to the view is that the management can pursue market transactions with suppliers and customers in an unconstrained manner. The existence of market forces will ensure that fair prices for goods will be taken.

So What Do We Mean By Stakeholders?

It can be argued that there are two forms of stakeholder:

those who are vital to the survival and success of the organization;
any group or individual that can affect or be affected by the organization, but do not have direct control.

The first group is the more significant. Let us look at how they impact on the organization, and divide the group up into its component parts.

Shareholders

Many would argue that shareholders are the only stakeholder group that really have any importance. They are, after all, the people who have the primary financial stake in the business and are therefore dependent on it (to an extent) for earnings. Furthermore, the money that they put in supports the business. Many more elderly shareholders need the funds from shares, unit trusts (which are just a 'basket' of shares) and so on when they can no longer work for a living during retirement. Of course, pension funds and other financial instruments will be based on the equity of companies. This is a significant point and brings us on to the next question. Who owns the shares? Traditionally, shares were owned by the owning family or some other close holding. For small private firms, this may well still be true, but for many large public corporations, this is no longer the case. Indeed, it is the nature of this shareholding that puts a big question mark over the view that a company should only be run for the shareholders' benefit.

These days, institutional investors own the shares in larger organizations. These include such things as pension funds. These are managed by fund managers who invest in equities to gain the best return for the funds that they manage. What this means in practice is that a significant percentage of the share ownership of major companies is owned by collective groups of individuals whose identity changes all the time. Certainly the company has a responsibility to these people, but whether or not this should be a sole responsibility is another matter. How can a company be solely responsible to a group of anonymous individuals who change on a weekly basis according to the views of professional fund managers? For this reason it can be argued that the shareholder model of the firm is too limited.

Employees

Perhaps, then, a company should have other responsibilities. Employees rely on the business for their livelihood and in many cases getting alternative employment may not be that easy. A company has a responsibility to these people and a major change in legislation over the past 30 years has been the increased protection in law for employees. Employees are a major group of stakeholders and a company certainly has a responsibility to them. In this book, we have already looked at human rights and the issues of capitalism and justice. Later on we will look at the treatment and rights of employees in other parts of the world.

A key point that can be made in this information-driven world is that with knowledge rather than effort being the main currency of business, it is the people who work in the business (and who have the skills and knowledge) that really count. Treating employees badly is very short sighted and will inevitably come to haunt us in the long run.

Suppliers

Suppliers are clearly vital to the success of the business and ultimately will determine the price and quality of the goods produced by the firm. There is much evidence that in today's competitive world, it is the ability to control costs rather than the ability to increase sales that really influences profitability. Increasingly the view is being taken that it is good relationships with suppliers that really count. We should certainly treat suppliers with respect.

A good example of this was the experience of Chrysler. This major car company famously almost collapsed causing massive redundancies – not just in the company itself but also amongst suppliers and distribution companies. One estimate was that the collapse would have resulted in 100,000 job loses. However, Chrysler survived. Much of the reason for its survival was that the suppliers all agreed to cut prices and take a long-term view when they were threatened. The building up of relationships between customer and supplier are clearly very important.

This factor has had a major impact in recent years. In particular there have been numerous cases where major companies have refused to use certain suppliers because these suppliers have acted unethically in their opinion. For example, Levi Strauss, the famous clothing firm, refused to use suppliers from China because of allegations of forced and child labour being used. We will look at this case a little later on in the book. Increasingly the view that 'we just buy as cheaply as we can' is changing to 'we buy from the supplier that gives the best overall deal'. More and more the 'best deal' will include an ethical treatment of its employees and other factors too. For example, the B & Q home-improvement chain in the UK has put a policy of only buying in wood products that come from sustainable forests. They are by no means unique in this policy. Of course, much will depend on the actions of consumers. If consumers demand ethically sourced products then suppliers will have to supply them in order to remain in business. What is clear is that increasingly companies will have to treat their suppliers with respect. They will have a responsibility towards the supplier as a stakeholder.

Customers

What about customers? Of course even defining customers can be difficult. Essentially a customer is someone that we serve and that can include a wide range of stakeholders. In this discussion, we are really talking about the people who buy our goods. The consumers of our products and services. Customers produce the lifeblood of the firm in terms of revenue. No customers, no business! It is worth noting that given the high level of reinvestment of revenue into development by most firms, then customers indirectly pay for new developments. What is clear is that closeness to the customer breeds success.

As we have seen in earlier chapters, though, there has been a tendency to treat customers with less respect than they perhaps deserve. The Manville case and others suggest that, certainly in the past, customers were regarded as people who could be exploited. There is still much of this attitude around today. As we will see shortly, the laws and views of customer care have certainly changed over the last 100 years or so and this has certainly put pressure on companies to treat the customer stakeholder with more respect.

There seems to be irrefutable evidence that companies that treat their customers well do better. The famous study by Peters and Waterman in the book *In Search of Excellence* pointed out that it was the excellent companies that really cared about their customers who won out in the end. Certainly you might make more money in the short term by 'conning' customers. In the long term though, poor customer treatment will catch up with you. This text is full of examples of this, from the Ford Pinto to the *Herald of Free Enterprise* disaster. It might be noted that several of the companies that Peters and Waterman held up as 'excellent', are no longer regarded as such. Perhaps we might also note that treating customers ethically is a very dynamic issue. We have to keep on scanning the environment to make sure that we keep up with the whims of customer demand.

The Local Community

This is another important stakeholder group. The local community gives the business the rights to build or rent facilities, benefit from the tax revenues raised in the area in the form of local services, infrastructure, and so on. In return for these services, it is reasonable that the firm should be a 'good citizen' and act in a responsible way. This might include the supporting of local charities, provision of local facilities and the sponsoring of local initiatives. There have been many cases where large multinational companies in particular have failed to do this and can be accused of exploiting the local community rather than supporting it. Many large organizations have considerable power – the very largest are the size of nation states – and it is certainly easy for them in many cases to abuse this power. We shall discuss this issue a little later in the book. What is clear is that organizations are part of the community and should act in a reasonable way.

The Environment

The relationship between the firm and its environment is also becoming a critical area. If we accept the shareholder view of the firm, we could simply say that it is the responsibility of the organization to make profits for the shareholders and that is it. If a company pollutes the atmosphere or causes some other environmental disaster, then that is the price that has to be paid for profitability. It can also be argued that if the consumer or society in general want a good environment, they should demand that environment through the market mechanism by voting for it with their money. Essentially, the shareholder argument would say that a company should basically produce what the market wants and maximize profits. It is not up to an organization to make socially correct decisions.

Increasingly, this view is being challenged. Many companies are taking a much more responsible view towards the environment and being proactive, not just reactive. We shall discuss this most important issue a little later on in the book.

Competitors

On the face of it, being responsible to competitors is a rather bizarre concept. After all, we are in business to make money and if we can knock a competitor down, then so much the better. However, are there no limits or rules to this? It can be argued that we do have a responsibility to competitors; that there have to be some rules and limits to anticompetitive action. Again, we will look at this issue a little later on in the book. I think we can conclude that again competitors are a stakeholder group, that we do, indeed, have some responsibility towards both from an ethical point of view and also a practical business one.

The Stakeholder Theory of the Firm

So what can we conclude from all of this? I believe we can argue that the conventional shareholder or stockholder idea of the firm is too limited in modern business. Certainly, shareholders are important because they provide capital for the firm. However, as we have seen, the loyalty of these shareholders may well be very variable. It is for this reason that we are advocating a move towards stakeholder theory.

The basic idea of stakeholder theory is simply this. Shareholder theory says that the purpose of the firm is to maximize the welfare of the shareholders subject to certain moral or social constraints, such as the laws of the land. This brings us back to the adage, 'if it's legal, it's OK'.

The stakeholder view suggests that the organization has a responsibility to a variety of interests, not just the shareholders. The firm develops and thrives by the maintenance of a number of relationships with these stakeholders. The company cannot survive without customers, suppliers, and so on. It can even be argued that good competition can make the business stronger too. There are countless cases of companies in monopoly situations that have become very inefficient because they had no rivals.

How Do You Put the Stakeholder Concept into Practice?

The starting point of the stakeholder approach is the setting up of a list of key values by which the business works. We can agree that the production of wealth is vital, but we might also note that the way in which these profits are produced is also important. The setting up of standards is vital. To start with the company would have to agree to certain limits that they would not wish to go beyond. For example, they might agree that lying to any stakeholder constituent is not acceptable. (We would include within this, of course, the concept of business bluffing.) We could also add to this that the company would not wish to carry out any immoral activity towards any of its constituent stakeholders, no matter what the reason. We might also suggest that the company may well choose to rule out activities that are currently legal because they are ethically unacceptable.

Green and others have suggested that to make stakeholder responsibility a practical proposition, a number of new organizational structures should be provided.

The Stakeholder Board of Directors

The idea of the stakeholder board of directors is fairly straightforward. It is suggested that most firms of any size, and certainly those, which are publicly traded, form a board of directors, which is comprised of stakeholder groups as well as members of the corporation. In simple terms as well as the usual members of the board, there should be representatives of key stakeholder groups as well. You might have a representative of a key supplier, a customer group and someone from the local community. These extra directors are vested with the duty to manage the affairs of the business in concert with the interests of the stakeholders. In many ways this is not a new idea. Many public organizations, such as universities and cultural bodies, already have this type of organization. However, for many private companies it can be a major change in mentality.

The Stakeholder Bill of Rights

This is an idea put forward by many protagonists of the stakeholder approach. The idea is reasonably straightforward. Each stakeholder would have the right to elect representatives and to recall representatives to boards. Whether this is done on a corporation-by-corporation or industry-by-industry basis is a matter for further discussion. Each stakeholder group would have a right to free speech, the right to grievance procedures. Essentially what you are doing is giving all of the stakeholders similar rights to the shareholder group primarily on the grounds that all of the stakeholders have a key part to play in the continuing success of the company.

Corporate Law

This is a difficult area because if we are accepting the stakeholder concept then inevitably corporate law would have to change. This is because traditionally corporate law has been very on the side of the shareholders. However, as we have seen, a number of developments over the past 30 years or so have begun to change things. The changes in employment law that we have already discussed have certainly made a difference and as we will see, changes in product-liability legislation and consumer responsibility generally have made further inroads into the traditional view that making money for shareholders is all that matters.

Perhaps a true stakeholder interpretation of the firm may be a rather utopian view, but the introduction of a stakeholder advisory board may be a possible compromise and many organizations are moving in this direction.

Consumerism and The Question of Product Liability

This is an area where there have been dramatic changes. To start with, we should go back in time to the middle of the nineteenth century.

Let's assume that you have bought something and you are not satisfied with it, for whatever reason. It could be that the product was defective, or far worse: it has ended up harming you even though you used it reasonably and followed any instructions that were provided. What could you do about this unfortunate situation? You might be surprised by the answer to this question.

In 1850, US law, and indeed the law of most developed countries at the time, stated that only those who could prove *fraud* or *breach of contract or warranty* could collect damages in the event that they were harmed in some way by a defective product. This in essence gave you very limited rights because satisfying the court's strict concept of fraud and breach of contract was very hard to prove. But that was only the start of your problems!

Who you could sue was also a major issue. Your options were only restricted to those people with whom you had a relationship of privity. This is a legal term that is not often used in everyday life and needs some explanation. In essence, privity means a *direct commercial relationship*. Let's assume that you bought something in a shop and it went wrong. You could only sue the shop – not the people who actually made the product even though it may have been their fault, and they were negligent and the shopkeeper may have been totally innocent. The thought process behind privity (which is still very much with us in agency law, incidentally) is that you can only sue the person with whom you had a direct contractual relationship. You did not deal directly with the manufacturer so you could not sue them. Of course, if you sued the shop then they could sue the wholesaler who could then sue the manufacturer and so on. Both of these factors made the whole process very cumbersome and impractical. There is no question that the power rested very heavily with the supplier.

This legal argument was further supported by a number of other economic ones. If we take the example of the period after the Second World War, this was characterized by being a time when the supplier held most of the power. Supply was limited and the demand from the newly liberated countries of Europe was considerable. There had been much devastation and rebuilding was necessary, again creating considerable demand. The supplier could get away with poor-quality goods and frequently did.

Things have certainly changed in more recent times. To a large degree, the idea of privity has been replaced by a new trend, a trend towards the doctrine of strict liability. Strict liability takes the view that it is the source of the problem that should be made liable, not the next in line in the chain. Invariably this has meant the manufacturer has had to shoulder the blame. Many would argue that this can only be right. However, the increased responsibility on the supplier has not been without its critics. The levels of compensation paid out to wronged customers, particularly in the USA, have been considerable and there now seems to be a move to redress the situation a little in favour of the supplier.

The real ethical point here is this. What is really fair? Clearly, we cannot have a situation where suppliers consistently produce unacceptable, if not downright dangerous, goods. On the other hand, if consumers can sue manufacturers for enormous amounts relatively easily, will this not serve simply to stop producers offering anything? As with most ethical problems, we are speaking about the drawing of a line.

The Development of Strict Liability

It is worth considering how the idea of strict liability, and consumer legislation has developed. This is perhaps best illustrated by looking at some milestone legal cases from the USA, a country where strict liability has perhaps been most developed.

Perhaps the first really significant case was that of *Green Man v Yuba Power Products Inc.* back in 1963. The judgment of this case was that the manufacturer has strict liability for damage caused by its products, even though the seller has exercised all reasonable care in preparation. In other words, the manufacturer is always inherently liable even though they have taken as much care as they could have done to make a product safe. If a customer sues them, the onus is on the supplier to show that they acted in a responsible manner. It is then up to the court to take a judgment of this and rule accordingly. A manufacturer cannot simply argue that the consumer did not use the product properly.

This concept was extended over the years with many more cases. In 1968, in the case of *Larson v General Motors*, it was ruled that when a faulty product worsens an injury, a plaintiff might recover damages for the worsened part of the injury, even if the design defect did not cause the original injury. In other words, if you were driving your car and had a bad leg and the car went wrong, caused you to crash and make your leg worse, the manufacturer could not simply argue that the plaintiff already had a bad leg, so they could not be sued. The court would rule that the manufacturer would be liable, albeit for the extra damage. They could not be held liable for the original injury.

Perhaps the most significant ruling, though, came in the next case. This was the case of *Micallef v Miehle Co. New York* in 1976. In this case, it was ruled that evidence that a plaintiff actually knew that there was a danger in using a product *will not* be a defence if the manufacturer knew that there was a danger and could have done something about it in the design. This ruling and many others like it have had a major impact on product liability. What it basically means is this. Just because a customer perhaps should have known that there was a danger with a product, this is no defence if the manufacturer did not take reasonable steps to point the danger out to them. Thus, we know that knives are sharp, but if a knife is particularly sharp, the manufacturer should point this out on the packaging. They cannot use the argument that 'it was obvious and the person should have known'. This has given rise to a range of anomalies and there is a view that the whole thing has gone to far. We will see comments on packaging such as a note on a packet of nuts noting that the contents 'will contain nuts'. Of course, nut allergies can be very serious – even fatal in some cases – so clearly warning labels are appropriate. But have things gone to far? What we are witnessing here is a major change. Traditionally, the view has been *caveat emptor* – 'let the buyer beware'. Increasingly the view is *caveat venditor* – 'let the seller beware'. One major implication of this has been the increase in the number of product recalls.

From the 1980s onwards, the number of products that have been recalled has increased dramatically. In the USA, the Consumer Product Safety Commission has the power to enact product recalls and in 1980 one car manufacturer, Ford, recalled more cars than it built. We will discuss this case shortly. Many retailers are also enacting product recalls to protect their customers, and in Europe the European Community is developing more and more legislation that supports the idea of strict liability.

Legislation globally increasingly requires that all household or consumer products that are declared unsafe must be recalled from the market and that all affected parties in the distribution chain – purchasers, retailers, distributors, and so forth, may be reimbursed. In the USA if a manufacturer is unable to recall products effectively – perhaps through lack of funds – the government is empowered to publicize that hazard in order to protect the consumer.

Total Quality Management and Business Ethics

What are the implications of all of this? The implication for suppliers is that they have to have a total quality system – there is no room for the 'cowboy supplier' of old. Total quality management – usually shortened to TQM – is an integrated approach within a business that aims to achieve continuous improvement in the quality of goods and services. This is achieved by getting everyone in the organization to work together towards producing a better-quality product. The key point of TQM is that everyone is responsible for quality: not just the quality-assurance personnel. The benefits of TQM are numerous and include:

- Improved customer satisfaction – giving the customer what they really want rather than giving them what we think they want.
- Better-quality goods and services that meet the needs of the customer accurately.

- Reduction of waste and stock so the business can become efficient and smooth running.
- More flexibility – the company becomes better at meeting customer demands, which are increasingly demanding.
- Reduced work in progress to improve cash flow.
- Improved and more accurate delivery times.
- Better use of the human resources in the business.

This is all achieved by the following strategies:

1. The development of a customer orientation – we give the customer what they want through a rational design process and competent marketing research.
2. Leadership by top management so that everyone in the organization pulls together towards the overall goal of customer satisfaction.
3. Statistical analysis of quality, problem solving and improvement so that problems in production processes can be identified and resolved.
4. The involvement of everyone in the business in the production of a quality product or service.
5. The recognition that multi-function work teams are the best way of sorting out quality.

Above all, everyone in the organization is responsible for learning, training and education, what is often known as 'the learning organization'.

So how are TQM and business ethics related? Both have similar objectives. Both have the overall objective of giving fairness to stakeholders and making the organization more transparent. It is easy to argue that the modern business needs to be both a producer of quality and a maintainer of good ethics.

The Development of Strict Liability

The development of strict liability has been dramatic, as we have seen. How fair is this approach? Have things gone too far? To answer this question we must look at the reasons behind the various judgments that have been made over the years in this respect.

Generally speaking, judges have justified strict liability using the following arguments:

1. Organizations have considerably more money than individuals and therefore it can be argued that if anyone is to be responsible for the quality of products it should be them. Besides, if there is a problem with a product, such as a product recall, it is the consumer who

pays in the long run anyway because the cost will be recouped through price.

2. There is a moral obligation for producers: if you offer a product or service on to the market, you should know what you are doing. Suppliers should be experts. We have seen how competition has made organizations improve quality and it can be argued today that if you are not prepared to enter the market with a quality product you should not enter the market at all. If you do offer a poor-quality product then you are being irresponsible and deserve everything that is coming to you. Of course, sometimes errors are made quite genuinely. As we have seen, strict liability accepts this, but takes the view that the responsibility is still with the supplier to show that they took every reasonable step to prevent problems.
3. Consumers cannot test products very easily. The alternative to suppliers being responsible for quality is to put the responsibility on consumers. They would have to test every product that they received. This is clearly absurd and comes around to the argument that consumers cannot be expected to be experts. In industrial markets, the situation might be a little different. Purchasers have had the means of testing products from suppliers and can set up specifications and so on. However, even this may be changing with the onus on quality in industrial markets now resting on the supplier, with incoming inspection and test slowly disappearing.
4. Having a policy of strict liability is certainly a deterrent to dangerous practices.

If a manufacturer knows that any attempt to hide behind excuses will fail in court then the manufacturer will go out of their way to ensure that things do not go wrong. Strict liability has undoubtedly increased quality.

The Future

Have we now reached a situation where suppliers are frightened to release products for fear of being sued by over-fussy consumers? Has consumerism gone too far? Have we gone to the point where if anyone is getting an immoral deal, it is the supplier?

These are good questions and a source of much debate, particularly in the USA. On 5 March 1999, the Senate Commerce, Science and Transportation Committee held a hearing on legislation to overhaul the product liability system. Although efforts to reform the system have been ongoing for almost twenty years, the legislation almost became law in 1998 before President Clinton vetoed it. In 1999, Senator John Ashcroft introduced a Bill identical to the Bill vetoed by Clinton. The Bill would rewrite the rules governing product-liability suits in state and federal courts, thereby bringing uniformity to the system. Perhaps most significantly, the Bill would *also place limits on the amount of punitive damage awards*. However, as we have seen, not everyone agrees. Opponents of the legislation claim the Bill would make it more difficult for consumers to gain redress for injury caused by faulty products and would diminish manufacturers' incentive to produce safe products. In other words the primary reasons for strict liability noted above would be undermined. One thing is clear: President Clinton has opposed the cap on punitive damages.

Should we cap punitive damages, or is the danger that if we do that, we let the suppliers off the hook and we end up going back to the days of *caveat emptor*?

Perhaps the best way of looking at this is to consider two very famous consumer cases. Both have gained infamy for different reasons. The first, the case of the Ford Pinto, happened at a time when the consumer did not have the power that they have today. The second, the McDonald's coffee scalding case, happened many years later when consumer power was far greater and to many people it is a good example of how consumerism has gone too far. However, you may not agree.

CASE STUDY – **The Ford Pinto**

Historic Background

Ford, along with the other major US automotive manufacturers, had always held a strong belief in the production of large cars. Henry Ford was once heard to say 'Large cars, large profits; small cars, small profits'. The availability of low-cost petrol in the USA supported this view. However, the oil crisis in the 1970s and the subsequent legislation on fuel economy that followed made Henry Ford's view untenable. Added to this, competition in the world car market was increasing. The dominance of local manufacturers in markets was under threat and Volkswagen in particular was making inroads into the US market. This competition was soon to be added to by the threat from the Japanese.

The response of Ford and General Motors was to develop smaller cars – the Pinto from Ford and the Vega from GM. Neither were the best designs and both were rushed. Lee Iacocca, then the President of Ford, was determined to produce a small car that weighed less than 2000 lbs for less than $2000. It was the desire to do this that ultimately proved to be the downfall of the Pinto. The car had a fundamental fault in that the fuel pump had been positioned in a vulnerable point just below the rear bumper. As a result of this, there was a strong chance that if the car were involved in a rear-end collision it would explode. Crash tests confirmed that this was a serious possibility. It would have been expected that Ford would redesign the car. The cost of this was calculated, but remarkably no corrective action was taken. The result was that Ford sent to market a car that was dangerous – and they knew it.

It is worth remembering that consumerism was far less strong in those days and communication far slower. It took some time for the realization of the Pinto's fault to become clear. Much of this was down to Ford's considerable power as an organization. The company had taken the view that it was cheaper to pay out compensation claims then fix the problem in the car.

For eight years, Ford used their power to fight off any attempts by government to change the fuel pump design, and they paid out millions in out-of-court settlements. Ford was selling 500,000 cars a year and making very high profits. In 1977 the magazine *Mother Jones* accused Ford of knowingly putting on the road an unsafe car in which hundreds of people had burnt to death. It was estimated that between 500 and 900 people had died needlessly. In the following year, on 10 August, two 18-year-old sisters and their 16-year-old cousin were hit from behind by a van when driving their 1973 Ford Pinto. The gas tank ruptured and all three were burnt to death.

The Elkhart County grand jury charged Ford with criminal homicide, the first case of an American corporation being so charged. It was during this famous case that an internal document came to light. This showed through cost-benefit analysis how Ford was indeed correct to keep producing the Pinto without modification. The analysis compared two things:

1. The cost of fixing the problem.
2. The cost of not fixing it and paying out compensation to people injured by the car – or to the relatives of those who died.

The analysis makes some assumptions about the level of compensation. The levels seem low by today's standards, but were realistic at the time:

Ford Pinto – Cost-Benefit Analysis

Savings: If we produce the car as per current designs, we can expect 180 burn deaths, 180 serious burn injuries, and 2100 burnt vehicles.

The cost of this will be based on the following levels:
Unit cost: \$200,000 per death, \$67,000 per injury
\$700 per vehicle

If we multiply these together:

Total benefit: 180 × (\$200,000) + 180 × (\$67,000) + 2100 × (\$700) = \$49.5 million

We should then compare these calculations with the cost of modifying the car:

Current sales levels: 11 million cars, 1.5 million light trucks
Unit cost to fix each car/truck: \$11 per car, \$11 per truck
Total cost: 11,000,000 × (\$11) + 1,500,000 × (\$11) = \$137 million

Thus it was considerably cheaper to kill or injure the people than to fix the car. In a remarkable judgment, Ford were found not guilty of homicide for the following reasons:

1. Ford could have kept out of the small car market and made bigger profits. However, the US market was under threat from foreign competition and Ford was doing a lot to combat this by producing the Pinto. Agreed, the car killed some people, and injured others, but far more people were kept in jobs as a result of Pinto production. It was more important to keep the Germans and Japanese out.
2. The Pinto met every fuel system standard in the USA and was comparable with other sub compacts. Here we see the 'if it's legal, it's OK' argument again.

These arguments were challenged and ultimately the case went to the Supreme Court who ruled that Ford should recall the car. In 1980, Ford recalled more cars in the USA than they shipped.

Analysis

The Ford Pinto case brings with it a wide range of questions. Perhaps the main one is *why? Why* would a major company release a car that they knew would kill people – indeed they even calculated how many – rather than fix it? It can be argued that they did nothing wrong because they did not break any laws. The car certainly met all of the regulations for sub-compact cars that existed at the time. However, as we have seen, this may well be a fairly hollow excuse. There may well be more than that. Pratley suggests that the company may well have suffered from a form of Groupthink. This concept (first mentioned in the famous novel *1984* by George Orwell and later developed by Janis and others) argues that a group of people will tend to focus on one objective and go along with the rest of the group in the search of this goal, even though the goal or the means should have been questioned. Essentially, people 'go with the flow' rather than question the action. The desire to bring out a car to compete with the Volkswagen product may have been so strong that any other consideration was simply ignored. The very calculations of the cost-benefit analysis reveal a great deal. The number of cars is greater than the number of burns cases, which in turn is greater than the number of deaths. Ford must have calculated how many people would be able to get out in time, how many would get burnt but would make it and who would be too slow! The cynicism of the whole thing is incredible if you think about it.

Pause for thought ...
How irresponsible were Ford in their release of the Pinto? Should they have 'gone back to the drawing board'? Consider the following arguments:

1. The car did not break any law.
2. By producing the car, Ford kept many people in work. The death of a few people was a small price to pay. Many other Americans lost their lives in car accidents during this period. It is best to benefit the majority.

Consider these ideas in the light of the ethical theory discussed at the beginning of this book. Can they be justified/supported?

There is no doubt that Ford used their considerable muscle to keep their Pinto case out of the courts. They put a great deal of pressure on the US government. The Pinto case, and many others like it, would tend to support strict liability in every sense of the term. Surely the consumer needs protection? But as we have seen, there is some question as to how far we should go. To contrast the Pinto case, let us look at another case, that of the McDonald's coffee scalding.

CASE STUDY – The McDonald's Scalding Coffee Case

This famous case occurred when Stella Liebeck of Albuquerque, New Mexico, was sitting in the passenger seat of her grandson's car and was scalded with hot coffee. She had ordered coffee that was served in a Styrofoam cup at the drive-through window of a local McDonald's.

After receiving the order, the grandson pulled his car forward and stopped for a short time so that Mrs Liebeck could add cream and sugar to her coffee. She placed the cup between her knees and attempted to remove the plastic lid from the cup. As she removed the lid, the entire contents of the cup spilled into her lap.

The sweatpants Liebeck was wearing absorbed the coffee and held it next to her skin. A vascular surgeon determined that Liebeck suffered full thickness burns (or third-degree burns) over 6 per cent of her body. She was hospitalized for eight days, during which time she underwent skin grafting. Liebeck wrote to McDonald's, seeking to settle her claim for $20,000, but McDonald's refused.

During the case, McDonald's produced documents showing more than 700 claims by people burnt by its coffee between 1982 and 1992. Some claims involved third-degree burns substantially similar to Liebeck's. McDonald's clearly had extensive experience with cases such as these. It transpired that, on a consultant's advice, the company had decided to hold its coffee at between 180 and 190 degrees Fahrenheit to maintain optimum taste. This is significant because most coffee is served at 135 degrees – McDonald's coffee was much hotter than the norm.

As the case progressed, McDonald's quality-assurance manager testified that the company actively enforces a requirement that coffee be held in the pot at 185 degrees, plus or minus five degrees. He also admitted that a burn hazard exists with any food substance served at 140 degree or above. This would mean that McDonald's coffee could not be drunk straight away. It would just be too hot.

A witness for Mrs Liebeck, an expert in thermodynamics as applied to human skin burns, testified that liquids, at 180 degrees, would cause a full thickness burn to human skin in two to seven seconds. Other testimony showed that as the temperature decreases towards 155 degrees, the extent of the burn relative to that temperature decreases exponentially. Thus, if Liebeck's spill had involved coffee at 155 degrees, the liquid would have cooled and given her time to avoid a serious burn. As we have seen, most coffee vendors offer coffee at lower temperatures.

McDonald's argued that most customers buy coffee on their way to work or home, intending to consume it there. McDonald's also argued that consumers know coffee is hot and that its customers want it that way. They accepted that their customers were unaware that they could suffer third-degree burns from the coffee and that a statement on the side of the cup was not a 'warning' but a 'reminder' since the location of the writing would not warn customers of the hazard.

In the event, the jury awarded Liebeck $200,000 in compensatory damages. This amount was reduced to $160,000 because the jury found Liebeck 20 per cent at fault in the spill. The jury also awarded Liebeck $2.7 million in punitive damages. It should be said that this amount, whilst sounding a great deal, only equals about two days of McDonald's coffee sales. In addition the punitive award was subsequently reduced to $480,000. The court noted, however, that McDonald's had been reckless and irresponsible, making coffee that was so hot just because it might improve the flavour.

Analysis

This is an interesting case. On the face of it, suing a company for huge sums because they produce hot coffee that is hot is bizarre. As we have seen, there is actually rather more than this to it and the lady was badly injured.

Pause for thought ... Could she not have expected a cup of hot coffee to be hot? How far should warnings go? Should there be a limit to how much compensation a company should have to pay out in cases like this?

One thing is clear, the power in business is now very much with the customer. It might be argued that this should be the case. We do not really want any more Ford Pintos – although in fact there have been countless cases in a similar vein since. Whether the power will swing back towards the supplier a little remains to be seen.

Obligations to Competitors

On the face of it, this seems a strange point to discuss. If we are in business to make money, do we really have any obligations to our competitors? Should it not be a case of anything goes?

It is true that, over the years, most free-market economies have imposed various legal restraints on competitive practices. Good examples of this are the antitrust laws in the USA. In addition, many countries have rules against price fixing or product dumping. These laws all aim to reduce economic power that would prevent market entry, drive out smaller firms or otherwise limit consumer choice.

In the USA, regulations enforce suppliers not to have preferential prices to favoured customers. We have also mentioned the work of the FTC about advertising regulations. The logic behind all of this is the notion that competition is the best way of giving the best deal.

As we have noted all the way through this book, there are laws and there are morals/ethics. What happens when competitors enter into practices that do not fit into any of these common categories?

There is a wide range of activities that happen between competitors that it can be argued should not. Good examples of this include raiding, sabotage and competitor-intelligence gathering. Let us consider these.

Raiding is a specialized form of competitor sabotage. Essentially, one company will aim to damage a sales promotion launched by one of its competitors by buying up the promotional goods. A well-documented case is that of Toys 'Я' Us and Child World. Essentially, Child World offered a range of goods at very low prices – almost cost price – and supported these with a range of gift certificates, which they gave to customers who spent a certain amount of money. Toys 'Я' Us concluded that it would make financial sense to buy these goods up, partly because the price of these goods was almost cost and also because it would damage the Child World promotion. Toys 'Я' Us thus sent their staff around to Child World in the lunch break and gave them money to buy the special offer goods up.

How acceptable is this? On the face of it, it looks like a clever business strategy. After all, it certainly combated the sales promotion of a major competitor. There was nothing illegal about the action either.

This is a simple answer but not a very satisfactory one. Certainly, we can note that normally companies try to protect against this sort of action by restricting the number of purchases that can be made – perhaps one per customer. Child World did not do this so you might argue that they were foolish. The problem with putting purchase limits on special promotions is that the person who loses is a legitimate customer.

One test that we have put into action throughout this book is Kant's universal rule – which relates to Green's NORM. If everyone did this, would that be acceptable? On this criteria alone, the action of Toys 'Я' Us falls down. If everyone was doing it there would be no sales promotions – or at least companies would have to take drastic action to combat competitor action. The real losers would be the customers. This is surely the point. Action like this ends up destroying the market for everyone. This is not a good thing.

Another technique mentioned above, competitor sabotage, is remarkably easy, which probably accounts for its popularity. Here are some examples:

1. A company hires a number of people to phone a competitor with lots of hoax enquiries with a view to tying up its people and phone lines and preventing legitimate customers getting through.
2. A salesperson puts a rumour around a small industry that a key competitor is 'having a few financial problems'. Nothing too specific – just enough to put doubts into customer's minds.
3. A group of salespeople at a trade fair visit competitors' stands. They have the following aims:
   - steal as much information and samples as possible;
   - steal customer leads if possible;
   - tie up competitor salespeople so that they cannot help genuine customers.

Clearly there is some illegality in the last case, but even this would be regarded as being acceptable in some industries. I have heard several sales managers tell their salespeople to go out and do just that. Essentially, it is a business-bluffing-type argument. Stealing things from people's houses is wrong, but stealing from other people's exhibition stands? Well, that is par for the course!

> Pause for thought . . .
> How acceptable are these actions? Can theft ever be justified? How about the other cases? These are not illegal but how would you justify their morality? What would happen if everyone did this?

Another technique mentioned above is competitor intelligence gathering. This sounds like spy versus spy industrial espionage. The truth is not far off. It is a growing area.

In 1986, the Society of Competitor Intelligence Professionals (SCIP) was formed and now has several thousand members. The SCIP has considerable credibility and defines competitor intelligence gathering as follows:

> Competitive intelligence (CI) is the process of monitoring the competitive environment. CI enables senior managers in companies of all sizes to make informed decisions about everything from marketing, R&D, and investing tactics to long-term business strategies. Effective CI is a continuous process involving the legal and ethical collection of information, analysis that doesn't avoid unwelcome conclusions, and controlled dissemination of actionable intelligence to decision makers.

It should be said that the SCIP do not advocate the breaking of any laws. In addition, they have a well-defined code of ethics. Not everyone is so scrupulous in their actions, however.

Intelligence-gathering equipment is freely available – there are stores in major cities such as London and New York where highly sophisticated equipment can be purchased. This has given rise to a number of ethical questions. Theft of competitor information is regarded as wrong by most; after all it is theft, but how about spying on people or hiring away people for information reasons?

A very common practice is for firms of consultants and others to ask graduate students to approach competitors posing as students looking for information for research purposes. The recent graduate will know how to sound like a student and can use this to gain the information that is required. Of course, this act is really a form of misrepresentation and it invariably muddies the waters for any legitimate students genuinely looking for information to complete projects.

It has been suggested by Green and others that there should be four basic rules of competitor gathering. In essence, there should be:

1. *No theft of documents or other tangible property.* Clearly, theft is illegal anyway, but as we have noted, many people in industry take the view that certain types of theft are OK in business. It is part of the 'industry rules', if you like.
2. *No deceit or misrepresentation.* This includes the student example above, as well as the hoax phone calls. There is a strong argument for transparency in all dealings in business. Again, if we apply the 'universal' rule, if everyone misrepresented himself or herself, what chance would industry have of survival?
3. *No attempts to influence the judgement of persons entrusted with confidential information (particularly the offering of inducements to reveal such information).* This is an interesting area. Clearly strong coercion, such as threatening someone with violence or blackmailing them, can never be right and is most certainly illegal in most countries (although common practice in some parts of the world).

However, influencing people can take other forms. Offering bribes might be a good example and we shall look into the whole concept of bribery later on in the book. There have also been many cases of potential-information suppliers having been taken to a bar and plied with drink to make them 'talk'. This is not illegal, but clearly the morality of such an act has to be questioned. How far can we really go?

4. *No covert surveillance.* This includes all of the spying already mentioned. Of course, this does go on. There are some issues to consider though. What do we mean by surveillance? Wire taps perhaps, but what happens if an individual overhears a competitor's employee discussing sensitive information in a hotel? Can this information be used?

I have put this question to many people over the years and almost all have said that they feel that using the information in this case would be acceptable. They say this for the following reasons:

- The information was not obtained deliberately.
- The people who were talking in the hotel foyer should have been more careful. It was their own 'fault'.

These are interesting answers and worthy of consideration. I would put forward the following questions: Why does the fact that the information was not obtained deliberately make any difference at all? Why do you have a right to the information just because you just happened to come across it by accident?

Consider this situation. You are walking down the street and find a suitcase full of money that is not yours. What should you do with it? Well, according to the law of most countries, you should take it to the nearest police station, *because it is not yours*. Most people would accept this – although some would certainly walk off with the money anyway. Now, what happens if the information that you heard in the hotel foyer is worth as much as the money in that briefcase? Should you use it?

Pause for thought ... What would you do in this situation? Why? Ask a group of your friends or colleagues what they would do. From my experience most people would use the information. How would they view the morals of such an act?

The Dangers of Competitive Action

Obviously, some responsibility has to be put on the people talking in the foyer. It was, perhaps, not the most sensible thing to do. Indeed, you could well argue that it is down to organizations these days to bring in as much security against competitive action that they can. But what happens in the case of some modern surveillance systems? It is now technically possible to eavesdrop on private conversations inside a building by beaming laser light on a window and recording vibrations made by the sound waves within!

Perhaps the biggest danger with competitive action is that communication – the basis of all business really – can be impaired. If everyone expects there to be sabotage and covert surveillance, then there will be no trust. As we have seen, trust is a fundamental issue in business.

Fair Treatment for Suppliers

As we have already mentioned, modern business practice is increasingly supporting longer-term relationships between customers and suppliers. The days where a major customer would simply phone around when they wanted something and the best price got it has largely gone. Increasingly, the supplier is seen as part of the value-creating chain of the customer. That said, there is often a high degree of ethical tension between suppliers and customers. Another major change in the past 30 years or so has been the polarization of business. The largest businesses are getting larger and being increasingly supported by the many smaller 'niche' suppliers that have appeared. Of course, by their very nature, the small companies are dependent on contracts from the larger companies and sometimes resort to unethical practices or illegal behaviour as a way of winning business. Purchasing managers often report that their most common problems are the offering of gifts and other inducements by supplier salespeople. We shall look into the issue of bribery a little later on in the book. However, bribery is only part of the problem. We might also list such issues as confidentiality. If two companies are going to work together then they need to keep critical information out of the public sphere. A very important idea today in business is the idea of 'knowledge management' – the management of knowledge by an organization using information technology. Increasingly customers and suppliers are sharing information using information technology in order to get the most out of this knowledge. In these arrangements, confidentiality is critical.

CASE STUDY – **Ben and Jerry's***

Ben and Jerry's was founded in 1978 in Vermont in the USA, close to the US/Canadian border. Ben and Jerry's philosophy is as follows. At one time religion was the force in society. Then it was government, now it is business. You can see this in the buildings in our society. At one time, it was the churches that most impressed us. Then large government buildings were put up. Today the most impressive of all are the head offices of major companies. Clearly business has a major impact on society and a major responsibility as a result. Ben and Jerry took the view that they could contribute a small percentage of profits to charity – but who would notice that? Their solution was to recognize that a large percentage of their $170 million-plus turnover will go through the business, and it is here that ethics could count. They have taken the view that they should act responsibly towards all of their stakeholders, particularly their suppliers. The company will, for example, use suppliers that do socially acceptable acts such as hiring homeless people or people recently released from prison. By the same token, the company would not use organizations that abused or exploited their employees.

**Summarized from the BBC's* Newsnight, *12 December 1997*

Pause for thought ... How socially responsible should a company really be? If a socially responsible decision cost the company money, should we do it? On what grounds?

Ethics in Sales

All sales and marketing activities raise basic ethical questions about the extent of our moral obligations to assist and inform the consumer. There can be little doubt that the personal selling function poses some of the most difficult dilemmas in business ethics. There are a number of reasons for this:

People in personal sales typically work on their own so they are not heavily supervised. If they wish to act unethically, it may not be that difficult to do. In addition, they often earn the bulk of their income through commissions. Of course, this generates pressure to close sales by any means as no sales means no income. Another problem is that there is often a disparity of information between buyer and seller, particularly in consumer-goods selling. This tends to create an opportunity for exaggeration and misrepresentation on behalf of the salesperson. It might be argued that this is less of a problem in industrial selling. Professional sales people will also point out that taking advantage of customers is a surefire way of losing your job in the long run. This might be the case, but if you are in a position where you have to get an order to make your monthly target up and you can do it if you act in some unethical way, what do you do?

There can be little doubt that in today's competitive business world, salespeople are always under pressure to sell more and achieve more. As a result of this, a key role of the sales manager is to motivate salespeople to achieve often very tough goals. Of course, if people are motivated there is always a danger that they push it too far. They achieve their goals but break ethical boundaries.

The traditional image is another issue of course. In the past, salespeople have been perceived as 'conmen' and 'carpet-baggers' who will do anything to make a sale. Without doubt, most of today's professional salespeople are not like that. However, ethics are subjective by definition and whilst there are many things that most people would say are either wrong or right there are many so-called grey areas in the selling profession.

Misrepresentation Versus Sales Puffery

A very important problem area in selling is the representation of products. There is a fine line between boasting and exaggerating a bit and totally misrepresenting a product to a customer. Although strictly this is a legal problem, it would be good to look at this before we move on to the ethically based areas.

There is often a fine line in selling between misrepresentation and sales spiel or 'puffery' as lawyers tend to call it. Misrepresentation is an objective statement about a product that is wrong. It is a lie – although even if you genuinely believe it to be true, if you give false information, you are guilty of misrepresentation never-the-less. Sales puffery is subjective views put forward by the salesperson to enhance the sale. For example:

- 'This car has done 20,000 miles' (it has actually done 80,000). This is inaccurate and misleading information and is misrepresentation.
- 'This is a great car.' This is the subjective opinion of a salesperson and is just sales puffery. What does 'great' mean anyway?

As we have seen, the line between misrepresentation and sales puffery can be small but it is one that salespeople have to be very aware of. Above all, it emphasizes the need for training. As we noted, even if you make a claim that you believe to be genuine, if it is not true then it is misrepresentation pure and simple. Product training is a must!

Whilst this is largely a legal conflict, it also becomes an ethical one if the salesperson deliberately misrepresents. There are many issues that a salesperson has to face that are primarily ethical in nature.

A common problem is where the ethics of the salesperson and the ethics of the corporation that they work for conflict. The conflict can be either way – either the salesperson feels that the company's ethics are weaker than their own or the company tries to impose a standard of ethics that the salesperson is simply not happy with. Much of this can be resolved through training and one of the tasks of the sales manager is to ensure that the salesperson is in line with the company on the ethical issues just as much as they are on product issues.

Another common problem is where the standards for one part of the organization are inconsistent with those of another. It is not uncommon for there to be one rule at the top and one rule at the bottom. For example, senior people such as sales directors may abuse expense accounts – making claims that were nothing to do with genuine business expenses perhaps – at the same time as telling junior salespeople off for making very minor errors in their expense claims. This creates an ethical conflict. Which set of rules is right? How can there be one set of rules for a senior person and one for the junior? This is a good question. I have put this question to many senior and junior salespeople over the years and the answer has often been along the lines that 'hierarchy' could explain this. Senior people should get a better deal than juniors. Perhaps, but do we not have to have general rules for everyone in the organization? Higher pay for senior people seems fair enough, but the right to bend the rules? Should not senior people set a good example to juniors as well?

Internal Conflicts in Selling

A serious difficulty can arise where an individual, rather than a business, has two ways of dealing with things. On the one hand the individual may have strong views about what is ethically acceptable in life. In reality, though, they may bend them a bit when it comes down to the actual order and justify their actions in some way. This comes back to the concept of business bluffing that we spoke about in an earlier chapter. The problem with this, as we have seen, is that the 'it's OK, really' line can be pushed so far that it is no longer OK at all. Also, strong internal conflicts can present serious health problems to the sales person in that doing something that you feel you have to do but also consider wrong can be very stressful. Many sales trainers and sales textbooks spend a lot of time these days on ethics training for salespeople. It certainly is becoming a key area.

Ethics in Sales – Some Specific Problems

As well as these general points we can also consider some specific issues that present common ethical problems to salespeople.

The giving of gifts and entertainment can be a very tough area for both the salesperson and the sales manager. On the face of it the basic idea of giving gifts and entertaining is not really a problem in itself but it does have a number of pitfalls. The basic problem lies in the motivation of the gifts. Most sales managers will say that the giving of gifts is nothing to do with 'buying' customers at all but merely rewarding them for their past business: a 'thank you' if you like. It may well be that the buyer is not bought with a gift but we have to face the fact that simply giving a gift to a buyer is putting them in a potentially difficult situation. Ethical business, it can be argued, should be made on the basis of price delivery and service. We will debate this in more detail later on in the book. Anything which adds to this price/delivery and service equation can clearly introduce anomalies. Most writers on the subject of sales would agree that the following three rules apply in most situations:

1. The larger the value of the gift, the less ethical it is generally considered. A free yacht is more likely to be a problem than a free drink!
2. Giving to customers is considered far more ethical than giving to potential customers. You can reasonably argue that if you take a current customer out you are merely thanking them for business that has already been placed and helping to cement a relationship between you. On the other hand, giving a large gift to a potential customer would seem to be a bribe by any standards.
3. Giving a gift that can be used at work is probably safer than a gift which is obviously meant to be taken home. Thus something for the office is probably a lot safer than a bottle of scotch.

But Why Give Gifts At All?

A typical reason for giving gifts at all is simply because buyers expect it. However, the picture here may be changing. There are many examples of major companies having rules, which expressly forbid their buyers to accept gifts – even a very small gift. If they do accept then they the buyer may be fired or, in some cases, the vendor may be struck off the approved vendor list. The issue here is that salespeople, and sales managers in particular, must be very aware of the policies of their customers.

Here are some thoughts to consider when giving business gifts:

- What are we trying to achieve with this gift? Is it to cement a relationship, or something more questionable? Do we really have to give a gift at all? Are we in compliance with the policies of the buyer's company?

- How significant is the gift in the overall sales strategy? Would we still get the order without the gift?
- When do we give the gift out? Should it be at work, at home or somewhere else?
- To what degree is the gift going to influence the buyer's decision? Is it literally the case that they would not buy unless we gave them a gift? Do we want to involve ourselves with such a situation?

Sabotaging Competitors

We have already mentioned this subject in the section about competitors. The salesperson has many opportunities to sabotage customers if they wish and there can be no doubt that every day salespeople do just that. One example might be where a salesperson who is allowed to look at the shelves of a store may 'adjust' the competitor's products a bit – moving them to the back or making their display a little smaller.

A situation that is sadly common is where a salesperson spreads a false rumour about a competitor or customers. This is very common and can be very damaging. It may well be that the rumour does not sound very likely. However, there is an old adage that 'there is no smoke without fire' and a company may have to work hard and long to get rid of the effects of such a rumour, even if they are not remotely true. Of course, it is easy to suggest that such comments are essentially slanderous. They may well be, but proving them may be difficult. In addition very vague but damaging statements may be made, such as 'I have heard that they are having a few problems.' The morality of it is a different issue. The concept does not seem to pass the 'universal rule' idea. If everyone were doing it there would be chaos in business. To some, telling stories such as this may well be seen as a form of business bluffing, something that you have to do to survive in business. I would suggest that such comments are never really acceptable.

Expense Reports

This is a major minefield for the salesperson and the sales manager. Selling is an expensive process but it is justified because it is highly effective at getting orders. In some types of business it is by far the most effective way. The salesperson is often given quite a range of company assets to do their job. A company car, perhaps a notebook computer, modem, mobile phone, and so on. In addition to all of these there will be an expense account. Most companies are not silly about expenses and rely on the salesperson to act in a reasonable way. However, the opportunity to take advantage of this situation is there, and it could result in very high sales costs.

Companies are generally working harder to ensure that the expense reports submitted are accurate and more and more detail is being asked for. One way of ensuring that expenses are correct is to repay them quickly to stop people using the money to float next month's expenses, or you can give a float.

The unethical – and frankly fraudulent – acts that expense accounts can generate are considerable. Perhaps the most common example is the salesperson who 'collects' receipts from all sorts of places in order to 'beef up' their expense claim. They may walk into a petrol station and ask the attendant to write them a bill, even though they have actually bought nothing at all. On the face of it, such action is fraudulent. However, the underlying mentality behind this might be considered. Certainly, there is often the view taken that the company almost expects their salespeople to exaggerate their expenses a bit.

The Problem with Financial and Other 'Essential' Services

Insurance agents and other sellers of financial products or services face a further problem. The complex nature of the product makes the client particularly dependent on the salesperson's expert knowledge and advice. Rightly or wrongly, customers view insurance brokers as being ethically committed to meeting the client's needs and to placing the client's interests above their own. The training that brokers get tends to reinforce this, emphasizing that a key factor in making a sale is gaining a customer's trust.

But insurance brokers are not doctors who study for many years in very strict educational conditions. Their loyalty is with the selling company and their foremost professional and personal goal is to maximize sales revenue. Furthermore, there are many stories of salespeople who work in these industries being far less well trained than perhaps they should be. It should be said that this situation has been tightened up in recent years in many countries. The basic ethical dilemma still exists. What should a salesperson do if to look after the customer results in less commission for themselves?

Again, the answer is one of balance. On the one hand, the buyer has to make some form of informed decision. *Caveat emptor* still has to apply to an extent. We cannot really see salespeople as being totally benevolent. However, clearly the salesperson does have some responsibility towards the customer, particularly in terms of not misrepresenting their offer.

Should a salesperson in an industry be forced to reveal their commission? This is an interesting question. On the face of it, it could be argued that if a customer knew which product made the salesperson the most commission it might assist them in making a more informed decision. On the other hand, you could point out that in most normal business situations we do not normally know the earnings of the person we are dealing with. You would not normally ask someone in a business meeting how much he or she stood to make from the transaction. That said, there is an increasing trend in the financial-services industry to state commissions.

The Use of Sales Techniques

Every sales textbook is full of sales techniques. In particular, closing techniques. The salesperson is told how customers tend to procrastinate and as a result it is the job – some might say duty – of the salesperson to use strategies to get them to buy. After all, usually the person needs the product and they are just a little uncertain whether or not to go ahead.

One problem with sales techniques is that they often involve the telling of untruths. For example, let's assume that you are a real estate agent, selling apartments. Sales have been slow but then someone walks in who is obviously keen. You take them around the apartment and they say that they want to buy but they would like to go away and think about it. What do you do? You have been trained to tell them that the apartments are selling fast and if they don't make a quick decision they might just lose the apartment. Of course, this is not true. Sales professionals would argue that all you are doing is encouraging the person to do what they want to do anyway. It is a 'white lie' used to give service to the customer. But who is to say that the person really does want the product or service? How does the salesperson know? Is lying – because that is what it is – ever justifiable?

An inability to close is one of the most common reasons for the failure of salespeople, so the use of techniques like this can perhaps be justified. However, if we once more apply the universal rule approach we might run into problems. What would happen if no salesperson told the truth? We would be heading for anarchy again.

> Pause for thought ... Have you ever had 'sales techniques' used on you? How did you feel? Were you pleased that they had encouraged you to do the deal or annoyed because they had tricked you with false information?

Sales is one of the most difficult areas in business ethics. There are a range of problems. The salesperson tends to have more knowledge and power than the customer, they tend to be commission driven and sometimes it makes more sense for salespeople to sell rather than tell the customer that the deal does not make sense for them. We can note that, increasingly, sales training is emphasizing both ethics and the long term.

The fact of the matter is that salespeople who take advantage of customers always get caught out in the end. Today the customer has a huge amount of choice and not only will they not come back, they will tell their friends.

Conclusion

This chapter has considered a wide range of issues in the stakeholder field. Above all, it has tried to answer the question, 'What responsibilities do we have to our stakeholders?' As we have seen, conventional wisdom suggests that the only real responsibility a company should have is to the shareholders. We know now that this is a rather limited view of corporate responsibility, although it certainly has its believers. The logical conclusion seems to be that whilst there are undoubted limits, the modern organization has a range of responsibilities of which the shareholders only make up one part, albeit an important one.

CHAPTER 7

Financial Ethics

Introduction

Finance and its various disciplines are another difficult area of business ethics. As we have noted, the Wall Street scandals of the 1980s were perhaps the starting point of business ethics as a subject. In this chapter, we will look at a number of different business ethics issues. To start with, we will look at one financial ethical area that has been with us a long time, that of creative accountancy. We will then look at insider dealing and then finally briefly consider the leverage buyout scandals of the 1980s.

Creative Accounting

It has been suggested that every company in the world is fiddling its profits and that every published set of accounts is based on books that have been cooked. This is perhaps an exaggeration, but there can be little doubt that creative accountancy is remarkably common.

Some forms of creative accountancy are well known. Examples might include the charging of private expenses to the firm's accounts in an attempt to reduce the individual's tax liability. One company director I knew used to reckon that his firm saved almost all of their salary bill because business expenses covered most of their day-to-day costs. For many, this may not be too unacceptable, although the morality and legality of defrauding the taxman might be questioned. However, other forms of creative accounting might be less acceptable. For example, the inaccurate stating of stock levels with a view to increasing or reducing profits is a common strategy. This can be used to reduce tax liability again or it could be done to make the company look more profitable or stable than it is. Stock is, after all, a significant component of assets in a company. But how acceptable is this manipulation? It can be argued that creative accounting is really a form of business bluffing and that the arguments for and against it are really very similar. We will look at some examples of creative accounting first and then consider the ethical aspects. It is worth noting that most creative accountancy is not illegal, and so the 'it's legal so it's OK' argument tends to come up again.

Why is Creative Accountancy so Common?

The basic problem is that the boards of directors of most companies are always under pressure to produce results which look good and help them retain their jobs. In addition to this, we have to say that the accountancy rules in many countries are just too grey. This means the rules are very much open to interpretation.

The days when a company's accounts were simply a record of its trading performance are no more. Why is this? There can be no doubt that the pressure to produce strong results is greater than before. We have already mentioned the ownership structure of modern public business and this is, without doubt, a contributory factor. As we have said, the majority of businesses are owned by large institutional investors. These investors are important stakeholders and publicly quoted businesses have to tailor their results to meet their demands. But who are these institutional investors? Well, they will include such organizations as pension funds and other fund managers. The managers of these companies will be looking to maximize the return of their investments both for their clients and their companies. Most types of investor are looking for a regular growth over a period of time. You might think of a pension fund as an example. In this case, progressive steady growth is needed. In reality, few businesses can achieve this and wide fluctuations are inevitable. Over time the net result will be the same of course, but the variations may unnerve investors.

A simple solution would be to 'smooth out' the performance of the company by holding back sales in certain periods and putting them through in others. This strategy is known as 'keeping things in the bottom drawer' and is remarkably common.

How acceptable is this? After all, it is a lie or an action that is intended to mislead. You might take the view that in the long run no one is going to get hurt and you are really just 'playing a game' – a form of business bluffing as we have said. What happens, though, if things start to get a little more questionable?

As well as a smooth growth curve, companies also have to live up to the expectations of the market. Most of these market expectations come from the big stockbroking houses that forecast the profits from a particular company and then use this projection as recommendation to buy or sell shares. These projections become a benchmark for the company. If the company fails to meet the projection then its rating inevitably becomes dented. Too many failures and the bottom may drop out of the market for the shares altogether. A company that has undervalued shares is very vulnerable to a takeover. Of course, there may be cases where the projection of the analyst was wrong in the first place. However, inevitably it is the company and not the analyst who ends up getting the blame.

Another contributory factor is short-termism. Investors often take the short-term view in investment and therefore look for companies that produce very good results there and then. Essentially, if you are a company that does not make optimistic noises about the future you may well end up with a low share price even if you are actually doing well. Most publicly quoted companies are stretched between telling the analysts what they want to hear and then actually delivering the results. If they do fail in reality then creative accountancy may well be the only solution.

Before we go any further it is very important to emphasize that creative accounting cannot make up for long-term poor performance. Creative accounting can really be viewed as a short-term approach to 'paste over the cracks' until longer term and more legitimate solutions can be found. Certainly, no amount of creative accounting will cover up for the fact that there is no cash to pay the bills. The basic idea of stock markets is that they are supposed to be about equal information but clearly this is not the case here. If information is misleading and some people are able to interpret it more than others, how can you have equality of information?

Some Specific Examples of Creative Accountancy

So how is creative accountancy done?

The manipulation of *fixed assets* such as buildings and machinery is a common strategy. A good example of this is the assessment of useful economic life. If you want to keep the balance sheet up then you can extend the 'useful life' of a fixed asset to the maximum. After all, who is to say how long a piece of machinery 'lasts'? Take the example of a car. Many companies keep cars for three years or less, but there is nothing to stop them keeping them for five years and extending the useful economic life. There is much evidence that creative accountants work the idea of useful life in reverse. Essentially they work out what you want to show and that dictates the life you put in!

A glance through any accounts text will show that there are different types of *depreciation method*. Perhaps the most commonly used are 'straight line' and 'reducing balance'. Which do you use? You can use either, but what is significant is that the choice can influence the balance sheet of the company. You are allowed to change from one to another and this can change profits. This is because with the reducing balance method you take a fixed percentage off each year – say, 30 per cent. In the case of the straight line, a straight-line graph is drawn between the initial value of the product and zero. In the former case, the amount taken off will be higher in the earlier years and less in the latter. In the straight-line method, the amount will be even throughout the life of the item. Swapping from one to the other will have an impact on the book value of the item even though it has not changed.

The area of current assets is perhaps one of the most commonly exposed to creative accounting. We will briefly consider a number of examples:

Stocks are one of the most commonly manipulated areas. The attraction for the creative accountant is that the value of stock and work in progress can be very subjective. Of course, the higher the stock at the end of the year, the higher the profits. It should be noted that this is a short-term effort because the next year's opening stock will be higher. What is clear is that stock can be valued in a number of ways – direct, with overheads, etc., and the actual value of older items can be a matter of opinion. How much is a half-used thing worth anyway?

One of the biggest problems experienced by companies that give credit is a bad debt. Small companies in particular often suffer from bad payers and perhaps this is really an ethical area of itself. However, debtors can also be used in the creative accountant's favour. All companies will have to make some provision for bad debts in the light of the comments above. The fact is though that this provision for bad debts can be varied. A result of this is that the higher the provision, the lower the profits and vice versa. Of course, this will sort itself out in the long run but it can certainly be used to smooth out balance-sheet changes from year to year.

Cash is another good area for the creative accountant. The amount of cash in the business can be manipulated by varying the timing of payments and receipts. Generally speaking, it is desirable for a company to have good levels of cash because it suggests liquidity. If a company wants to show high levels of cash in the bank at the end of the financial year then it will make sure that money is banked and that outgoing payments are held back. It may even chase up debts and offer incentives for fast payment. Of course, as soon as the balance sheet is drawn up, payments are made and the debtor policy returns to normal.

In most accounting methods, earnings per share exclude extraordinary items (which are related to events outside the normal business of the company) but include exceptional items (which can be expected to occur from time to time, but not too often). To boost share values, a creative accountant will try to keep costs down by calling them extraordinary items. This is a very good example of how accounts can be very subjective in nature.

There is a wide range of creative accounting techniques but whilst many are noticeable there are several that are not even visible to the most highly trained eye. This is known as *off-balance sheet accounting*. This is where, rather than trying to amend figures, you actually leave them out completely. A common reason for it is to obtain funding which the company would not have otherwise been able to achieve. It might be that a company needs more funds to carry on but debt levels are too high. One of the great ironies of business is that the more money you have, the easier it is to borrow it – and yet the less you need it. Companies that really need the money often cannot borrow it because they are, on paper, a bad risk. Creative accounting may be the answer.

One way of doing it is to set up a company that is controlled by the initial company but not a subsidiary of it. A subsidiary in law is defined in terms of the ownership of equity or the ability to control its directors. How can you control a company but not own it? Remarkably, there are several ways in which this can be done. One way is to set up another company that has different directors but agrees to do what the other company does. So you might appoint your Aunty Mabel (who is 85 and does not really care) as a majority shareholder and director and you just tell her what to do. Transactions can be set to allow the transference of debt to this company.

As an alternative, the new company's shares could be split into a voting and non-voting shares on an equal basis. Although all of the shares are part of the equity of the company, only the voting shares actually have any power. Naturally, the holding company has the voting shares and therefore controls the company, even though it does not have a majority shareholding.

How acceptable is this? On the face of it, it is very deceitful and there have been many attempts to stop off-balance sheet accounting around the world. Sadly, various forms of it are still common. You could, of course, take the view that all of the creative accounting techniques are just good examples of sound business strategy. After all, if you can get away with it, why worry?

So How About the Auditors?

An auditor is employed, in theory, to protect and act on behalf of the shareholders. However, the primary role of the auditor is to claim a true and fair view. Providing this has been achieved, it is often difficult for an auditor to take much action. There are other problems too. Generally speaking, the audit marketplace is mature and much of an accounting firm's income is likely to come from consultancy work. As can be imagined, no firm wants to lose a client. There will inevitably be cases where if creative accountancy is not supported, valuable business will be lost. This is not saying that the auditors act improperly or illegally, but where there is a matter of judgement then the auditor may sway towards the client. This situation is getting worse as competition increases. In the USA in particular, it is noticeable that there is a growing trend towards action against auditors who act in an improper way and in some cases firms may even be sued for fraud or negligence.

Creative Accountancy and Government

So far we have talked about the private sector. The public sector is also suffering from creative accounting. Many of the major companies are now privatized, of course, but it is interesting to look at some figures from the past to illustrate how creative accountancy is not just restricted to the private sector.

A well-publicized example of governmental creative accountancy occurred during the Thatcher era in the UK. The electricity industry was hit during its financial year 1984/5 by a bitter miner's strike, which ended up as being a conflict between the government and the mining industry. The Thatcher government was keen to show how damaging the strike had been to the nationalized industries and was disappointed to hear that the electricity industry had only made a small loss of £146.6 million during the period: clearly, this would not make a great headline. In the event, the loss reported was £1277.1 million. This was a much more serious amount and it supported the government's claim that the strike had been very damaging.

The reason for this much higher figure was yet another form of creative accounting. Most accounts are prepared using the historical cost convention, which means that the costs in the books are as they were when they were first bought. The only problem with this is that it can be argued that an inflated profit performance is shown. This is because many of the items in stock would probably have cost a lot more if they had been bought now rather than in the past. This is particularly the case during inflationary times. The alternative approach is to build in a figure for inflation to costs. This is known as current cost accounting. Naturally, a company that changed from historical cost to current cost would show a much larger loss and that is exactly what happened here. The electricity industry changed its cost convention from historical to current cost and subsequently increased its loss dramatically.

International Creative Accountancy

Sometimes, creative accountancy comes about because of opportunities across currencies. One of the most common strategies is that of currency mismatching. On the face of it, this is a simple idea. You borrow money in a low-interest currency, such as the Swiss franc, and then invest it in a high-interest currency. You then pocket the profit! Of course, there is a catch. When you convert the high-interest currency back to Swiss francs, depreciation in currency value has reduced your profit to zero. But what happens if you publish the 'profit' on the interest and hide or delay the loss on the depreciation? This will result in a large profit – at least for now.

A famous case of this was that of Polly Peck, a company that had grown dramatically during the 1980s and whose share price had risen from that of a penny a share to a much higher level. The company had showed an enormous profit for the year ended December 1989. However, this was a complete illusion because borrowing in hard currencies and investing in the Turkish lire, a currency that had very high interest rates but was depreciating rapidly, had made the profit. The foreign exchange losses as a result of this depreciation were not put through the profit and loss account, but were declared in the balance sheet. The result of all this was that Polly Peck was able to declare a £12.5 million income, after borrowing £530 million. The losses from the depreciation were noted on the balance sheet but were essentially hidden. These misleading accounts led Philips and Drew, a subsidiary of the Union Bank of Switzerland, to lend Polly Peck £7 million. Polly Peck subsequently went bust in 1991 and Philips and Drew never saw their money again.

It should be noted that the accounts presented were audited. However, they were perfectly correct even if it could be argued that they were bound to mislead. In reality, Polly Peck was probably looking to simply smooth out a bad period in trading – a common reason for creative accountancy, as we noted. The net result was the same.

I am now going to look briefly at two other areas of financial ethics:

Insider Dealing

In simple terms, insider dealing occurs when an individual with inside information about a company – say, because they are an employee or director of that company – uses their particular knowledge to gain on the stock market. The information is not available publicly and may have come second hand. It might be that the person knows someone who works for the company in question, perhaps. A simple example of insider trading might be this. An employee might know that the company is about to gain a very large order. This might well push up the share price. Should they go out and by the shares?

As a result of the scandals in Wall Street and other markets in the 1980s, insider dealing is illegal in most countries of the world. However, it still goes on and low-level insider dealing is remarkably easy to commit, as we will see. Perhaps the most likely people to be accused of insider trading are the directors of the company. Their position puts them in a position of trust within the company and therefore it is expected that they will not use the information for their own gain.

The principle underpinning stock exchanges generally is that all investors have access to the same level of information. Thus if one investor knows something, then everyone should. An insider dealer has privileged information and therefore an unnatural advantage. A good example of this was the case of Michael Cowpland, Chief Executive Officer of Corel, the Canadian Software Company. Cowpland was charged with insider dealing by the Ontario Securities Commission. The charge related to his 1997 stock-trading activity. Essentially, he had sold off 2.4 million Corel shares for the total price of $20.5 million one month before the firm reported an unexpected loss. This loss resulted in a massive drop of the shares and nearly 40 per cent was knocked off the company value. Cowpland answered the allegations by stating that he had needed the money to pay off personal loans. Cowpland was actually charged with tipping information to his holding company, telling them that Coral's shares were going to drop, insider trading, and also making misleading or false statements to the Commission.

At the time of writing, the investigation is still continuing. What is clear is that the revelation has been very damaging to Corel and irrespective of the outcome, the future of Cowpland at the company has to be in doubt.

It is easy to argue that the specialists who work in brokerage firms also have unequal information. How else could they make a living? It might be noted that the Securities and Exchange Commission in the USA has charged many brokerage firms and commercial banks with insider trading. Of course, most people when they talk about insider dealing are referring to high-level corruption. However, it is very easy for an average employee to inadvertently insider deal. Let's look at two examples:

A group of middle managers meet at lunchtime in the company restaurant. They discuss business and one, who is in sales, mentions that they are about to get a larger order that will mean that the company will far exceed the current performance predictions. They all agree that they ought to buy some shares in the company. It turned out to be a good decision, because the price went up and they made a reasonable profit.

A printer is asked to print some company accounts. They have not been officially released yet. The chairman's report notes that the company has done far better than expected. The printer notes this and goes out and buys some shares, which duly rise.

Pause for thought ... How would you deal with these issues?

Leveraged Buyouts

This was one of the great ethical issues of the 1980s, and is worthy of consideration because it illustrates well some of the basics of financial ethics. Furthermore, as we have noted, it was one of the problems that first prompted the subject to come to the fore. The term 'leverage buyouts' refers to a variety of transactions concerned with mergers and acquisitions of corporations. The term leverage – or gearing – refers to the amount of equity money put into the transaction. Essentially, a leveraged buyout has a large amount of loan capital involved. Loan capital is generally cheaper than equity, but it has its problems. A highly geared company with lots of loans is very vulnerable. An increase in interest rates can make the business inviable.

This in itself is a problem, but the real issue at this time was the method of financing the deals. Many transactions were funded with what were known as 'junk bonds'. These were essentially 'IOUs': unsecured debts based on the promise of paying a hefty interest rate. Of course they were very risky because they were only based on a promise rather than anything more tangible.

There are many forms of leveraged buyout. The transaction may result in a publicly quoted company going private by individuals buying out the public shareholders, or a company might be merged with another corporation. Often the management of the company will look to buy out the business from the public corporation.

Leveraged buyouts are not new in themselves, but the examples in the 1980s had a number of features that made them stand out and create some major ethical questions. A key issue was the reason behind the takeover. On the face of it, takeovers occur because one group of individuals believes that they can run a business better than the current group. One of the features of the 1980s buyouts, which is still used as a motivation, is the concept of synergy. The idea is that by combining the two businesses in question, the net result will be greater than the sum of the whole. This is often called the '2 + 2 = 5' concept. There are many good reasons for believing this idea. Economies of scale should happen because of the increased size of the business and there will be redundant assets that you can put to use elsewhere. For example, you will not need two sales offices or two human-resource departments any more. By combining the best of both companies you will get better performance and with fewer people.

And yet the synergy argument does not tend to work in reality. The majority of mergers have not achieved the required aims, and 2 + 2 is more likely to equal 4 and possibly even 3½! Indeed, during this period many companies actually made a very good living by splitting up existing businesses. A good example is the Hansen Trust group.

The second issue concerned the amount of money in the takeover and the way the project was financed and the huge profits made. The fact is that only a portion of the money raised in these takeovers and mergers were actually for the takeover. The rest ended up with brokers and other financial institutions in the form of fees. This would seem to be a strange phenomenon. How can you justify realizing all this extra cash? The main reason given was this concept of synergy. The resulting company will, supposedly, be greater than the sum of the parts and will have a far greater growth potential than the old companies. This growth will ensure that the recipients of the investment will be more than able to repay the debt and high rates of interest on the junk bonds. A frequent argument put forward is that the value of the company being purchased is far higher than the quoted stock-exchange value and it is assumed that the price is understated, usually because the business could be better run. How viable is this argument?

The evidence is not that good. As we have seen, synergy is an elusive animal. The reason for this is that synergy assumes that the two businesses can work together, that they will be compatible and that it will be a good marriage. The divorce rate in many countries has now gone over 30 per cent and this seems to be a similar problem in mergers and acquisitions. Different cultures within organizations inevitably mean that you are more likely to get clashes than cooperation. For example, if two companies are merged on an equal footing, who is in charge of whom? If one company has a very flexible structure and management style and the other is very rigid, how do you sort that out? As might be expected, there is little evidence that the economy of most industrialized nations has gained as a result from these takeovers.

So why were these takeovers so popular in this period? A key reason was the deregulation of the stock market. In the USA, the decision was made by the Securities and Exchange Commission to remove the fixed rate on stock transactions for brokers and make it negotiable. There was much evidence that this rate had been artificially high and, of course, as soon as an open market was declared the revenue from stock transactions fell. In the UK, the so-called 'big bang' had similar effects. Leveraged buyouts were one way of regaining this fee base. It might be noted that the largest leverage buyout during this period, that of RJ Reynolds and Nabisco, generated around $1 billion in fees for those who actioned it!

Another factor is the tax position, which in the USA and in many Western nations typically favours debt rather than equity and dividends.

The Dangers of Leveraged Buyouts

These buyouts had a number of problems attached to them.

1. The companies created by them were not always an improvement on their constituents and, because of the way they were taken over, had large amounts of debt capital. Weaker companies were being produced.
2. The fear of takeover resulted in managers running businesses for the short term. Indeed, it can be argued that the power of the market over the running of companies generally has had a detrimental effect on organizations in the long term. High cost, long term and variable pay-off items will suffer. This might include, for example, new product development and R&D. These are vital strategies for most organizations, but may not produce a short-term return. As mentioned throughout this book, the typical shareowner today is not the proprietor who might have taken a long-term view but the institutional investor.
3. It can also be suggested that the paper entrepreneurs, people who make money out of money, are wasting their talent from a societal point of view. Surely the world would be better off if these people used their talents in the form of creating real products or services?

The Buyback

Leverage buyouts were very much a 1980s concept, although as we have noted, they do seem to be coming back and some of the activity that led up to the South East Asia crisis of the mid-1990s does seem to have come from similar forms of dealing. More recently, a new phenomenon has been seen, known as the buyback. The idea of a buyback is very straightforward. You purchase your own shares out of the organization's resources. At one time no company would have bought their own shares back as it would have been seen as weakness. The view would be that they didn't know what to spend their money on!

The idea behind share buybacks is that they are an obvious way for a company to increase shareholder value and provide something to do with their cash. When business conditions are strong, companies have a lot of cash. This poses the question, what do they do with it? They could certainly invest it by buying other companies, but often in boom times these companies are probably overpriced. It would be far better to wait for more difficult times and purchase a company that was struggling for a bargain price. Very often, it makes more sense for them to buy their own shares.

During the late 1990s, a long list of companies entered into share repurchase programmes. For example, Rank spent £142 million on 4.9 per cent of its share capital, pushing up its share price by 2.2 per cent. In the USA, 1475 US companies announced a record $177 billion buyback of stock. Why might buybacks be an ethical issue? The trouble is that whilst the concept seems acceptable on the face of it, it is open to abuse. There are three main factors to consider:

1. The controlling shareholders in a PLC can use the buyback artificially to support their share price and thereby make dishonourable gains. If you already own shares in the company and then use your management position to bring the price up, is this really an abuse of your position and power?
2. Another problem is insider trading. People who know about the buyback in advance can buy shares and gain as a result. If you are in a position to make a buyback and also own shares, is this not an abuse of your position?
3. A controlling shareholder might use buybacks as a way of consolidating their control and fending off a hostile take-over. This might well be thought of as an acceptable action by management. However, it could also be deemed unethical because it creates an artificial situation where a company that should have been bought out is not.

As we have noted, the problem with buybacks is there is an inherent opportunity to insider deal. A good example of this is the case of 3Com. This Californian company was faced by a class action filed by Atlanta-based law firm Chitwood and Harley, which alleged that the company and some of its officers violated the 1934 Securities and Exchange Act by using company money to buy shares in order to boost the stock's value. It was alleged that the net result of this action was that the directors of the company were able to sell their shares at an inflated price. The inflated price, of course, was caused by the action of the directors. Essentially they were accused of using the company's money to increase the value of their own shares.

On investigation, it was found that between 1 September 1998 and the end of December 1998, $130.4 million was spent on buying back 4.3 million shares and during this time the share price more than doubled from $23 ⅛th to $51 ⅛th. Concurrent with this, insiders within the company were selling large number of shares at prices as high as $48.69, or around double the 'pre-buyback' price. Soon after this, the company's sales declined and the share price dropped to $22¾.

CASE STUDY – **Rogue Trader: The Nick Leeson Incident**

The Nick Leeson incident was perhaps the most celebrated financial case of the 1990s. Leeson worked for Barings Futures Singapore (BFS). He had been hired back in 1989 in the lowly role of bank-office clerk but had progressed quickly up the ranks. By 1992 he was in charge of both trading and settlement in Singapore on the Singapore International Monetary Exchange. His success had been considerable. Indeed, he delivered over half of the £52.9 million in revenue for his division in 1994 on his own. The award-winning trader was regarded as a 'miracle worker'. Unfortunately for Leeson and his bank, his luck ran out. Perhaps overconfidence led him to gamble on the Nikkei 225 Stock Index. He had bet his reputation and bonus on the fact that the Nikkei would rise. He also made some predictions on interest rates. In the event, he was wrong in both cases. The market continued to fall and his losses mounted. He attempted to cover his losses by hiding them in the now famous account number 88888. However, the market fell further. Nick panicked and fled the country. In the event, the 28-year-old Leeson managed to bankrupt Britain's venerable Barings Bank with a mountain of debts. He was eventually arrested in Frankfurt en route to London. After eight months in a German jail, Leeson was extradited to Singapore, where he was promptly arrested at the airport.

On 1 December, Leeson pleaded guilty to two charges of cheating connected to Barings' $1.4 billion loss and was sentenced to seven years in prison. Leeson's losses exceeded £700 million ($1.2 billion) completely bankrupting Barings Bank. In the event the Dutch bank ING bought Barings Bank for £1 and commenced a rescue mission.

Analysis

The reason for the Nick Leeson incident has been discussed in great depth. It is generally agreed that the bank had been negligent in giving their 'star' trader too much freedom. There was a clear lack of segregation within Leeson's duties, which meant that it was easy for him to cover his tracks. If other people had been working with him, the real situation might have been made clear more quickly. A lack of supervision was also clearly a problem. Another point that was very obvious was that nobody questioned the unusual profits he was making, and when queries were raised the bank did not seem to investigate the case in much depth.

To many, the Leeson incident suggested that the greed of the 1980s was alive and well. Nothing had changed. The Far East at this time had been very buoyant – the Asian Crisis was yet to be experienced – and it could be argued that the conditions that Leeson faced were not very different from those of the mid-1980s in the USA. Certainly he had seen considerable success and overconfidence may well have been a contributing factor. Who is to blame for this incident that brought down an old and well-respected bank and put many people out of work?

Clearly, Leeson has to take much of the blame. It was interesting to note how the attitude of the media changed during the case. Initially he was seen as a 'loveable rogue' but as the enormity of what he had done came to light the view began to change. Many now saw him as an irresponsible fool. However, not all of the blame can be laid at his door. The company was also culpable, as we have seen. It is an interesting and important question to ask, in the event of a wrongdoing like this, who is responsible? Is it the individual themselves or the company as a whole? Does the company have a responsibility to ensure that the chances of something bad happening are as low as possible? This important issue will be discussed a little later on in the book when we consider the issue of corporate responsibility generally and some relevant cases.

Conclusion

Financial ethics are amongst the most complex for any company. As we have seen, it was a financial ethical incident that really started the whole subject of business ethics in the first place. Business is all about money and there will inevitably be cases of individuals acting in an unethical way. Increased controls and education seem to be the solution in both cases. There are a large number of grey areas in the financial area that could be firmed up, and it is without doubt that the increased public awareness of this sector in the past two decades has made a big difference.

CHAPTER 8

The Ethics of the Environment

In this chapter, we shall look at so-called 'green' issues. These have become a key discussion point since the 1960s and they certainly provide an important question for today's ethical manager. We will attempt to consider the following key issues:

1. What exactly are 'green' or environmental issues? This apparently simple question is not that easy to answer and requires some thought.
2. Who should be responsible for environmental issues? Can we just pin the blame on government or should other people be involved?
3. What are the implications of environmental problems? What is going to happen if we carry on as we are right now and do not take sufficient action?

Let's start with the first question. The truth is that 'environmentalism' seems to have a multitude of meanings. For example, we might include in our list: the disposal of industrial waste; the saving of endangered species; the conservation of energy; preserving the ozone layer; and many others. Some people might go further and suggest that vegetarianism is also a green issue. Who is to say that they are wrong? This vagueness is one of the big problems with environmentalism – defining what an environmental issue is. To be frank, it might be better to concede that there are so many possible green issues, it is difficult to see what is *not* green.

To make things still more complicated, we can be green in some ways and not in others. How about recycled paper? Is this green? You would have to say 'yes', but it may well have taken vast amounts of energy and a long truck journey to get it to your home. Non-recycled paper might have come a shorter distance and not required as much energy to produce. The fact is that many green products are environmentally strong in some ways and very weak in others.

Another important question is this. Do people really care about environmentally friendly products anyway? It would seem so on the surface. A well-publicized survey at the end of the 1980s when environmentalism was beginning to become a key issue certainly supported this view. In 1989, the Michael Peters Group, a US consulting firm, found that 89 per cent of Americans were concerned about the impact of the environment of the products they purchase, and more than half said they would decline to buy certain products out of a concern for the environment. Perhaps most notable of all, 78 per cent claimed that they would pay more for a product packaged with recyclable or biodegradable materials.

The problem is that this is not borne out by supermarket sales. True, some products such as organic foodstuffs seem to have sold well, but any supermarket buyer will tell you that many environmentally friendly products do not sell that well. You might consider this question. How often do *you* recycle your waste? When was the last time that you went to a bottle bank or recycled your waste paper? Perhaps you *are* very good at this, but most people, frankly, are not. Why might this be?

A lot of it probably comes down to the market mechanism. There are no real financial incentives to be environmentally friendly, nor are there massive penalties if we are wasteful. This is bound to change eventually, and we will discuss this view later. We might add that in parts of the world where incentives have been put in, there has been some success. A good example is the case of the Seychelles. This tropical island paradise clearly has a major incentive to keep its environment as clean as possible. At the same time, its inhabitants are one of the highest consumers of beer in the world! The hot climate also makes the consumption of soft drinks considerable as well. The potential for large amounts of waste is obvious. The solution has been to go back to glass bottles and add a large deposit value on each one. As a result, consumers return the bottles to the store. The local children, who are grateful for the 'returns' money, rapidly gather up any that are left around!

Once we have agreed what we mean by green issues – and that is not always clear, as we have seen – we need to ascertain who is ultimately responsible for the environment. Ronald Green and others have suggested that there are essentially three groups who could be made responsible. As with all ethical discussions, there are no clear-cut answers, but it is certainly worth considering the evidence. Three possible responsible groups are:

1. Government: local, national and international.
2. Organizations and companies.
3. The consumer.

Let's look at these in turn. How about governments? This would seem to be a very logical choice. After all, governments have the power and influence to get things done. They could tell both of the other groups what to do, and pass laws that would make environmental damage illegal. Certainly there is some environmental control by legislation. For example, some industrial waste is controlled by legislation and in the UK the cost of pollution control is estimated to be around 1.5 per cent of GNP. In some countries the figure will be higher. The problem is that legislation is difficult to enforce, often because of the very vagueness of green issues that we noted. How can you enforce something that you are not really sure about? Incentives to encourage both consumers and industry to be greener are often discussed and there is also the possibility of introducing taxation that discourages pollution and other environmental issues. The debate over GM crops is perhaps a good example of where government intervention has taken an environmental stance – primarily as a result of consumer and media pressure.

Government policy can sometimes be well-meaning but have the wrong effect. A much discussed example is that of the Amazon rain forest where state subsidies distorted economic choices and artificially favoured forest clearance in place of more sensible policies that would have resulted in conservation. Given that the Amazon Basin stores two thirds of all the earth's fresh water, this is clearly a concern.

The view taken by most governments is that they should aim to strike a balance between environmental benefits and the costs involved. In simple terms, more could be done but it would probably result in higher costs, and these would have to be paid for in taxes. This brings us on to the next issue: that of vested interest.

The vested interests that influence governments are a key factor in this discussion. Many contributions for political parties come from big business, and unpopular legislation could result in the loss of support. A good example of this is the so-called 'road lobby'. This includes car manufacturers, the oil companies, transport companies and major building contractors. The power of the road lobby in the UK cannot be underestimated. It argues that cars give the consumer choice and freedom, and that the only solution to transport problems is to build more roads. It argues that trains and other forms of public transport are unreliable and unpleasant to use. The road lobby gained a great deal of support in the UK from the Thatcher government, primarily because the alternative was the highly unionized public-transport sector. This support may not be quite as strong as it was at the present moment, but the undoubted power of pressure groups, from whatever direction, cannot be doubted.

Governments have also been involved in the environment at the world level and we will talk about this a little later on in this chapter.

What about companies? If a company discharges waste into a river, then surely it is their responsibility to tidy it up? The 'making the polluter pay' argument is very compelling. Indeed, the view can be supported by economic theory. It can be argued that polluters are basically avoiding their true costs because they are not paying for the cleaning up of pollution. Ultimately, someone will have to pay for it. Why not the organization that causes it? These extra costs are what economists call the external costs of production. There have been many cases of producers being influenced by Green Pressure Groups, such as the boycott of CFCs.

Having said that, there is little to suggest that most big business wants to be green really. A famous and much publicized study by Amitai Etzioni of Harvard Business School found that over two thirds of *Fortune 500* companies had been charged with serious ethical crimes, and many of these involved the dumping of hazardous wastes. A cynic might suggest that the others had not yet been caught.

We have to make the polluter pay! This seems like a strong rallying call, but there are problems with it in practice. We should consider some of these. The first problem that we come up against is this: how do we actually catch companies and make them pay? Over the years, companies have managed to find loopholes and ways round pollution legislation. One classic case was that of McDonald's who claimed that their packaging was 'CFC free'. However, it was actually made from CFC-22 which is a chemical derivative of the same chemical family. They managed to get away with it because of a legal loophole. The US Environmental Protection Agency said that CFC-22 is technically not a CFC, although its effects on the ozone layer are identical to chemicals which are formally recognized as being CFCs. We might note that the CFC-based plastic was a cheap option and its use reduced costs for the company.

Let's assume that the companies can be caught. Compensating the people who suffered can be a difficult question, as it is not always clear who they are. Often, there are direct sufferers but what about future generations or people in other countries who are indirectly effected? If your pollution spreads over several hundreds of miles, who do you compensate then? Equally, if you pollute the ground and the effects of this pollution last 200 years, who do you compensate? All of those generations? Do you allow for inflation?

Putting a price on environmental damage is a real problem too. How do you put a price on repairing the hole in the ozone layer? By using cost-benefit analysis, a compensation level can sometimes be arrived at. Even then we might have some problems. What happens if the polluter says that they are competing with rivals and the cost of a clean up will put them out of business? You might end up suing the company, giving compensation to a group of people and putting the very same people out of work because the sued company cannot continue. Sometimes, setting compensation claims can be a problem because of international differences – the famous Bhopal case, discussed later on in this book, is a case in point.

But should a company ever have to pay for environmental damage? Some writers such as Friedman argue that a company only has one reason in life, to make profits for its shareholders. On this view, going green only makes sense if it is profitable. If we accept that, then the sacrificing of profits in favour of the environment is fundamentally immoral. For Friedman the central principle is ownership. The shareholders own the business and the managers are acting wrongly if they don't maximize profits come what may. Others agree. Former US President Ronald Reagan famously argued that trees should be seen as commodities controlled by market forces. If consumers want them, they will pay for them. If not, so be it.

So perhaps the solution is that the green issue should be consumer led? After all, market forces are very strong and we are all very aware of the adage 'the customer is king'. It seems another compelling argument. Get consumers to buy environmentally friendly goods and you will resolve the environmental problem. Manufacturers will have no option but to produce the goods. If consumers do not demand environmentally friendly goods, then how can the manufacturers be expected to supply them?

There are problems with this argument. First, to say that all businesses look at customer demand and then provide it is rather limiting. Traditional marketing theory would suggest this but in reality many businesses do *create* wants through promotion, and patterns of consumer behaviour can be changed. It is not just a case of 'giving them what they want'. Sometimes they don't know what they want. Anita Roddick of Body Shop fame has a very simple business policy based on the assumption that the public is capable of being educated to think in an environmentally sound way. If you educate them, they will buy. How can they be expected to buy green products if they are not actually offered the products in the first place? One problem with this is that the consumer can be easily misled.

Two classic examples will be mentioned to illustrate this point. One is that of British Rail who decided to show their support for the growing environmentalist movement by labelling all buffet-car paper napkins with the term 'recyclable'. This is not the same as recycled, although the two words could be easily mixed up. Of course, most paper can be recycled. What they were really doing was saying 'these napkins are made out of paper'! An even better example is the well-publicized advertisement put out by AEG who claimed that their dishwashers saved newts (a small lizard-like member of the frog/amphibian family which is endangered and protected in the UK). The reason for this amazing claim was as follows. AEG appliances are slightly more energy efficient than their rivals. They therefore use less energy. Less energy production means less acid rain, and acid rain kills newts. Of course this argument was bound to have a major effect on consumers. How many of them actually bought the washing machine because it was good for the small amphibians has never been calculated. I think we can conclude that the advertisement was somewhat misleading, though.

What is Going to Happen?

There are several views at present. One can be summarized as the doomsday scenario as put forward originally in the Forrester Meadows model. This is the fundamental argument of many environmentalists. The crux of this argument is simple. Our environment, the earth, is finite in resources and therefore growth cannot continue indefinitely. This means that we have to make some trade offs. Above all, the argument goes, if we carry on the way we are right now, the whole thing will 'blow up in our faces'. Doomsday will come. Let us take arable land as an example of this. The earth has around 3.2 billion hectares of arable land. This sounds like a lot but in fact only around a half of this is under cultivation and to use the rest, according to UN data, would not be particularly economic. The average person in the world needs the food from around 0.4 hectares of arable land per year to survive (the average US person needs around 0.9 hectares!) and many will live on far less than this. Given that that six billionth person on the planet has now been born, some simple maths will show that we could have a problem.

Predictions made in the 1980s suggested that the world would be facing serious food shortages by the year 2000. Even if food production could have been increased four-fold, there would be a big problem by 2030. Essentially each doubling of production will give us just 30 years.

Of course this assumes that there will be no further development of urban cultivation. So what has happened?

Rather than getting worse, the food situation seems to be getting better. Without doubt, hunger is still a problem. It is estimated that 24,000 people die each day from hunger or hunger-related causes. However, this is much lower than it used to be. In 1990, the figure was more like 35,000. In 1980, the figure was around 41,000. However, this does not mean that there are not substantial problems. Childhood hunger is certainly a problem. Around 10 per cent of children in developing countries die before the age of 5. Again though, the number is down 28 per cent as compared with the period soon after the Second World War. The primary cause of hunger, it should be said, is not really a lack of land but a lack of resources. People basically die of poverty. Poverty leads to malnutrition which leads to death from the diseases which most target the hungry. It should also be noted that around 800 million people in the world suffer from hunger and malnutrition without actually dying from it. Food is undoubtedly a problem, but we might note that improved food productivity has not made the prediction come true. What is perhaps of more concern for the future is water. It has been predicted that in the twenty-first century, it will be water that poses the greatest resource challenge to the planet.

Global Warming

On 13 October 1997, the chief executive officer of the Exxon Corporation, Lee Raymond, told the 15th World Petroleum Congress held in Beijing:

1. The world isn't warming.
2. Even if it were, oil and gas would not be the cause.
3. No one can predict the likely future temperature rise.

Geologists using sophisticated carbon-dating techniques and other research have proved that the earth has both warmed and cooled before. The period we are in now may well be one of the warmest for some time. It could be argued that the phenomenon that we call 'global warming' is just a temporary 'blip' in the natural way of things. This is certainly the view put forward by the Exxon representative. But there are many others who disagree with this view, as we will see.

The theory of global warming is quite straightforward. The so-called greenhouse gases – including carbon dioxide and methane – build up in the atmosphere. Where does this come from? Essentially, carbon dioxide is the most important of the greenhouse gases that are generated by human activity – primarily through the burning of fossil fuels. The gases trap the sun's heat in the earth's atmosphere, instead of allowing it to dissipate into outer space. The result of this activity is that the earth will warm up.

But how reasonable is this view? Despite the comments made by Exxon's chief executive officer, the evidence to support this view is strong. Perhaps the most compelling evidence is that the amount of carbon dioxide in the atmosphere has risen by 30 per cent since pre-industrial times (about 1750). The evidence shows that temperatures are rising. This is the view of the IPCC. The IPCC are the United Nations Inter-government Panel on Climate Change, and are generally believed to be the world authority on global warming. They were founded in 1988 and are comprised of more than 900 scientists from 40 countries. The IPCC has produced many papers and reports. Here are some of its findings:

1. How warm will the earth get? The estimate of the IPCC is that global surface temperatures will rise by 2 to 6 degrees F or around 1 to 2 degrees C by 2100. Temperatures have risen by around half a degree F since the late nineteenth century. The view is that global warming is going to become a major problem in the future.
2. In its report of 1995, the IPCC stated that: 'The balance of evidence suggests a discernible human influence on global climate.' So it seems that human-created global warming is caused by human beings rather than by natural variation.
3. If global warming continues, crop yields will fluctuate, improving in some areas and plummeting in others. Overall, global agricultural production probably won't change. The sea level is projected to rise between 6 and 38 inches. A possible increase in extreme weather could batter coastlines and cost lives. The warming could cause 'significant loss of life'.
4. Improvements in energy efficiency of between 10 per cent and 30 per cent are feasible at little or no extra cost. Gains of between 50 per cent and 60 per cent are possible in some areas. There are many options for reducing greenhouse gases, but some depend on lowering the cost of alternative technologies.

The twentieth century was at least as warm as any other since 1400 and the last few years were the warmest on record. The picture has been distorted a bit. Going back to the speech of Lee Raymond, he pointed out that satellites have suggested that the earth is cooler than twenty years ago. However, the IPCC says that this is misleading, because satellites do not measure the temperature on the ground, and this is what matters.

The Kyoto Summit

The Kyoto summit of December 1997 brought representatives from 159 countries together. The resulting pledges were not what many environmentalists wanted. The deal was as follows:

The USA is to cut emissions by 7 per cent by no later than 2012 and the European Union by 8 per cent by the same date. However, the US Senate is heavily against the reduction of emissions and the deal is unlikely to be ratified. Perhaps even more significantly, there was not even theoretical agreement from the 136 countries not currently required to make any reduction, that they would have to made reductions eventually.

The effects of carbon dioxide will kick in properly around 2050. We face very significant warming in the far north of the planet, which will cause seal levels to rise further. There will be serious floods, droughts and a much higher incidence of malaria. The Meteorological Office calculated that there would be four times as much carbon dioxide in the Earth's atmosphere by 2100 – 30 per cent higher than previous forecasts. Scientists blame some of the increase on the continuing devastation of the rainforests by timber merchants and developers. This not only robs the planets of trees, the most effective way of converting carbon dioxide into oxygen, but also leads to 'die back' in which more carbon dioxide is released into the atmosphere by the rotting trees.

Ute Collier, a World Wide Fund for Nature delegate at the 2000 global warming summit in Bonn, said, 'This is quite frightening. It's not just the heating up, it is the extreme weather events which have trebled in number over the last 30 years. Events like Hurricane Mitch and the cyclone in India will happen more and more.'

Climate Change – the Consequences

Food Poisoning

There is a strong relationship between food-borne illness and temperature. If temperatures increase, we may see a growth in food-poisoning cases.

Air Pollution

Climate changes could lead to the production of photochemical pollutants (e.g. ozone). This could result in an increase in asthma, respiratory diseases and allergic disorders.

Foreign Diseases

Air-borne diseases found in tropical regions (e.g. malaria and dengue fever) may have wider spread due to climate changes. This could increase transmission of diseases not currently seen in the UK.

Seasonal Health

There may be an increase in sunburn, skin cancer and cataracts due to increased sunshine hours. A wetter winter climate may lead to unhealthy housing conditions (condensation, mould and overheating).

Extreme Weather

An increase in extreme weather (e.g. floods and storms) could lead to an increase in deaths and injuries, as well as contamination of water supplies and sewer systems.

Seasonal Mortality

There could be a decrease in winter deaths owing to fewer cold spells and an increase in summer deaths owing to heat stroke and hydration, especially in the old and the young.

Water Quality

Higher water temperatures and decreased river flow could lead to poorer water quality. Water shortages could lead to contamination of drinking water.

Shellfish Contamination

Contamination of shellfish with marine biotoxins could increase because of higher water temperatures. When ingested by humans, this could lead to poisoning.

Mineral Depletion

There is a serious possibility that many minerals will run out within the next 40 years.

Pollution Absorption

The ability of the world to absorb pollution is reducing. We only have to look at the death of Lake Erie and of swordfish in the USA owing to mercury poisoning to see that.

What Are We Supposed To Do About This?

Fundamental to the solution is the 'cradle-to-grave' audit. A truly green economy would require that all products should be audited for their effect. This is often known as the cradle-to-grave approach and looks at:

- The value to society of the good (i.e. product).
- The cost of transport.

- The cost of disposal.
- The long-term investment plans of the country.

Is the Doomsday Scenario Reasonable?

Some argue that the doomsday scenario is unreasonable for the following reasons. It does not take into account the price system. The price mechanism is, above all, a means of allocating scarce resources. This can impact in a number of ways. At the moment, the cost of labour is a very significant cost of production. On the other hand, natural resources cost on average only around 5 per cent of the costs. Therefore the impetus is on labour cost reduction rather than on raw materials. However, we can suggest that as the earth's natural resources run out, the motivation to reduce raw material costs should become stronger and therefore the currently low productivity of resources should be increased.

Another factor of the price mechanism is the substitution effect. If a resource becomes scarce then other resources can be substituted, as they are now cheaper. It can be argued that consumers will be pressed into buying fewer resource-orientated goods through the price mechanism. Advocates of the price mechanism also argue that pollution could be controlled through this method. The basic problem, they argue, is that a scarce resource, the capacity of the earth to act as a waste disposal, goes unpriced or certainly under-priced. To correct this, polluters should be charged through taxation and other measures. This will do three things:

1. Make pollution-intensive goods expensive.
2. Make pollution-intensive processes expensive.
3. Generate revenue which we can use to clean the earth up.

Advocates of the price mechanism argue that putting a limit on emissions in a factory is rather peculiar. What you are saying is that it is fine to pollute the earth up to a point, and then after that point the cost is infinite! The main view of the price mechanism school is that they feel that the doomsday scenario misses the fact that there are many things that we can do.

The 'food running out' argument is also popular. Work by the WHO and the UN suggests that modern cultivation methods and the increased use of soya and similar crops could reduce the pressure. Perhaps the biggest threat now, as has been mentioned, is not so much food as water. Significant shortages can be expected to develop during the course of the twenty-first century.

I think we have to face the fact that the goal of zero discharge is probably a dream; the cost of saving the first 50 per cent is much lower than the second.

CASE STUDY – **The Body Shop**

Anita Roddick opened the first Body Shop in Brighton in 1976 with the help of a loan of around £4000. She had no previous business knowledge and had no formal business training. She is well publicized as saying that her success was primarily down to the fact that she never went to business school. Roddick believed that the beauty industry sold false dreams to women by offering expensively packed products for skin care – products that have little or no benefit at all. In particular, Roddick believed that ageing women will pay astronomical sums for products that give very little value and yield massive profits to the cosmetic companies.

In response to this she started her own shop, selling a range of 'natural' cosmetics, shampoos and related items. Her primary target market was members of the so-called hippie counter culture, and much to her surprise, she had considerable success. For the next ten years, the company grew dramatically both in the UK and abroad. Body Shop now has 1407 shops in 45 countries with retail sales of around £750 million. Roddick has become a multi-millionaire.

Campaigning against animal testing was the Body Shop's prelude to educating the public in other areas of environmental concern. In 1985, the Body Shop sponsored posters for Greenpeace, and used its shops as campaign platforms to raise public awareness about endangered species, promoting awareness of AIDS, acid rain and the diminishing ozone layer, among others. Perhaps the biggest success was the company's rain-forest promotion where Roddick sourced some nut oil from the Kayapo Indians for her hair conditioner. Roddick became known as the 'Mother Teresa of Capitalism'.

More recently, the picture has begun to sour. In particular, there have been many apparent cases where the claims made by the Body Shop were not in fact true. Questions were raised about the 'natural' state of the products. It was claimed by several test laboratories that the company's products were actually full of petrochemicals. Its support of charity has also been controversial. The company claimed that they gave away 'an inordinate amount of pre-tax profits to charity'. However, it was found that the company had in fact given nothing to charity during its first eleven years and has given on average far less than the average company over its history.

The company has expanded greatly by franchising. This is not a problem in itself, but the unethical nature of its franchising agreements has come under considerable scrutiny over the years. Body Shop has been sued by several unhappy franchisees and the US Federal Trade Commission conducted a 16-month investigation into the organization.

One of Body Shop's strongest strategies has been its 'Trade not Aid' programme, in which it promoted the development of fair trade by using ethical sources for its products. However, it has been suggested that this only represents a very small percentage of turnover in reality. In recent times, Roddick has been accused of being a fraud and a modern-day colonialist.

Some of Roddick's strategies have caused public concern. In March 1998, Roddick caused more controversy by planning to sell skin creams made out of the cannabis plant hemp. Roddick is a leading supporter of a campaign to decriminalize the drug. John Keogh of Parents Against Drug Abuse said: 'What they are doing is legal but youngsters will put two and two together and come up with five.' In the summer of 2000, the UN warned that promoting hemp products was part of a campaign to legalize cannabis by making it seem 'innocuous'. Asked if the Body Shop seemed to be advocating the use of cannabis, Ms Roddick said: 'Absolutely not. We're talking about commercially grown hemp.'

Analysis

Despite all of the problems experienced by Body Shop, it is hard indeed to ignore the considerable success of Roddick in building her cosmetics empire. The real question is her true motivation. Is she an ethical idealist or a businesswoman who saw a considerable 'niche' opportunity in the market? Does she really practise what she preaches? The jury has been out for some time on this question.

Conclusion

The main questions that we have to face are these: what is going to happen if we carry on as we have been doing, and who is ultimately responsible for the protection of the environment? Neither question is easily answered. What we can say is that the environmental issue is likely to be a very significant one in the future and that a variety of agents are going to have to work on the problem to ensure that the best results are achieved.

CHAPTER 9

The Ethics of Globalization: Ethical Relativism

Most of our discussion so far has assumed that we are operating in one country and along one set of cultural lines. What happens when you are dealing across national and cultural boundaries? In simple terms, do ethics change with the border of the country? Do we just put away our morals and start using someone else's? It is well known that culture varies a great deal around the world and we might well question who are we to impose our cultural standards on others? It might be argued that whilst there are transcultural values, ethics really will vary around the world and we should act accordingly.

Perhaps one of the best approaches given to this is that by Pratley (1995) who suggests that we should distinguish between norms and values. He defines norms as 'specific expectations about concrete behaviour'. He describes values, on the other hand, as 'abstract collective representations of what people believe to be just, good and worthwhile to pursue'. In simple terms, values are what you believe in and norms are the way those beliefs are expressed.

It would be very simple to suggest that since every culture has its own set of rules there can be no overall guidelines for human beings to follow. In other words, 'when in Rome, do as the Romans do'. Should we always accept the actions of others?

I would suggest not. There are many things that go on in other parts of the world that we may find unacceptable. It could be argued that we have no moral right to interfere with the actions of others and that also we should have a respect for the cultures of others as well. However, should we accept a flagrant breach of human rights? Should we accept people being tortured or enslaved? We should certainly accept the fact that different cultures have different ways of doing things. It is the 'things' that we have to concern ourselves with. This brings us back to the norms and values argument. Our norms may differ but some basic values should not change, irrespective of where we are and whom we are dealing with.

This discussion takes us into the very difficult area of international ethics. The international businessperson has a range of problems to address. The primary one is the fact that they have their own set of values and norms which they have to relate to the values and norms of people from other countries and cultures. How should they deal with this?

This problem becomes worse when we look at multinational companies. These are often based in developed countries with developed country rules and mentalities. However, the countries that they are working in may well be very different. How should they handle this? There are two approaches to the problem. One is to take the view that a company or individual should always follow the standards of the country that they are in right then. If the standards are clearly lower than the country that they operate from, so be it. Often, these lower standards present an excellent opportunity for the individual or company to save money by cutting corners. This idea has been dubbed 'the ethical chameleon approach' because it suggests that the corporate strategy adopted is to follow the rules of the country that the company is in, irrespective of the standards present at the company's base. Thus, whilst a company would never dream of using or attempting to use child labour in their home base (the local laws would probably not allow it anyway) if they can do this in another country, and it is morally and legally accepted there, why not? It should be said that many companies have fallen foul of this argument in recent times and, irrespective of the morality, we might argue that being an 'ethical chameleon' can never be a strong strategy in the long term.

The alternative approach is to take a unitarian view of ethics and morals and argue that there can only ever be one set of rules irrespective of the situation faced. You cannot simply change the rules according to the location you are in.

Low-cost Labour

CASE STUDY – Guess in Mexico

On 15 July 1999, the National Interfaith Committee for Worker Justice released a new report called 'Cross Border Blues', which detailed the conditions uncovered in factories then producing garments for Guess in Tehuacan, Mexico. Guess has been accused of having sweat-shop conditions in its factories in Los Angeles, and of paying wages well below the national minimum wage. However, the report found a much bleaker picture in the company's factories in Mexico. The findings included:

1. Those workers were being forced into taking unpaid overtime. The report gave the following reason for this: because workers were given unrealistic daily production quotas to meet, they often had to stay late to complete their work. Furthermore, they were prevented from leaving the factories – in some cases by armed guards – until they had finished their quotas. In some factories producing for Guess, workers had to work all night to complete their quotas. Many workers report that they are not paid anything extra for working overtime.
2. Guess has been accused of paying low wages in the USA and this problem seemed exaggerated in Mexico. The workers interviewed during the study reported earning the equivalent of $25–54 a week. To put this in perspective, the cost of the market 'food basket' for a family of five in Mexico as of June 1997 was about $69 a week.
3. Living conditions for workers are also poor. Typically they live with their families in one-room, dirt-floor shacks without electricity or running water.
4. There were reports of workers even younger than 14 being used. It should be said that compared with some countries this age is relatively high. In some countries children as young as 5 or 6 have been used.
5. Often, women are given pregnancy tests when applying for work and are not hired if the test is positive. The thinking of this is that they will be unable to work in due course and might become a burden on the organization.
6. Fines are common. Many workers have excessive fines deducted from their pay if they take time off due to illness.

7. Workers report frequent accidents as well as health problems due to high levels of dust and poor ventilation. Injured workers are expected to get themselves to the government medical centre, paying their own way on public transportation.
8. Workers report instances of armed guards accompanying supervisors on their rounds. Some supervisors yell at, curse and insult workers. Some push or hit them.

Pause for thought ... Which of these conditions would you say is acceptable, which is not?

Analysis

It could be said that working conditions like these are common for this part of the world and that Guess are at least offering these people work. Furthermore it could also be said that they are not forced labour. If they don't like it they should go elsewhere. We might also suggest that using cheap labour like this is Guess's response to market forces.

Competition is tough and the consumer is ever powerful. To keep costs down and give the customer what they want, cheap labour has to be used. The arrangement basically faces economic reality. If conditions were improved, the cost of the jeans would go up and this would make the factory unprofitable. Inevitably this would mean that Guess would have to go elsewhere. You might also argue that Guess's role as a business is to maximize its shareholders' wealth and using these low-cost workers is surely one way of doing this. As far as responsibility is concerned, it might be argued that the Mexican government should be responsible for the workers who are the citizens of theirs. Should Guess care about what their customers think? Perhaps, but we might conclude that most consumers don't really care about where their jeans come from anyway!

How reasonable would you say these arguments are? Would a stakeholder approach be more appropriate here?

Child Labour

The idea of small children working in dangerous conditions for wages that are clearly exploiting them is not acceptable to many. And yet many poor families in the developing world have no option but to send their children out to work in order to make ends meet. In addition to this we might argue that whilst going to school would be the best option, if there is no school available and none likely in the near future, then sending children out to work at least gives them a useful existence.

To many in the developed world, the idea of child labour is totally abhorrent. On the face of it, children should be spending their time in school or at play. Working in a factory or out in the fields would seem to be the last place that they should be. But for millions of the world's children, work is the norm rather than the exception. In India, where child labour is particularly prevalent, it has been estimated that between 60 and 115 million children are at work. It should be said that this estimate (that comes from the Human Rights Watch report of 1996) is far higher than the official Indian government estimate – but most people would agree with this high figure.

What type of work do the children do? This is very varied and ranges from agriculture to manufacturing and services. Some of the work is undoubtedly unhealthy (if not downright dangerous), including working in brickworks or with machinery. Many of the children are what are known as bonded labourers – working to pay off debt in almost slave-like conditions.

Why do these children work? The obvious answer here is poverty. Many of the poorest families in the developing world lack the resources to survive without the extra money from their children. Research by the International Labour Organization has shown that in many cases the children bring in around one third of household income. Families in the developing world do not normally have access to welfare payments or the ability to borrow money.

Are child workers being exploited? Children are paid less than adult workers for the same amount of work, and are undoubtedly viewed as a low-cost source of labour by many employers. Is child labour legal? Often it is not. In India, the constitution outlaws child labour under the age of 14, for many types of work. Unfortunately, enforcement is a big problem with such a massive population.

What is the Solution?

Education seems to be a key factor. Making education compulsory and improving literacy is undoubtedly a major solution. In Pakistan, for example, child labour numbers in the sportswear factories have been reduced enormously by making education a compulsory requirement. Up until the mid-1990s, stories of children working for up to 80 hours a week in virtual darkness were commonplace. The signing of the 'Atlanta Agreement' – a voluntary act by manufacturers to stop using child labour and inspections by the International Labour Organization – have reduced child labour dramatically. However, reducing the levels of child labour is not always easy to achieve, as the loss of work often reduces income levels and forces parents to put their children back into the labour force. In addition, where child labour has been cut, manufacturing costs have risen. It is estimated that the cost of producing a football in a Pakistani sportswear factory has gone up from 25 rupees to 40 rupees as a result of these measures.

Pause for thought ...
Is child labour really a problem, or is it simply the case that people in the developing world see it as a problem because it goes against their beliefs and values?

How acceptable is child labour? Can it ever be justified in your view?

Multinationals – Purveyors of Dreams?

The term 'multinational' is perhaps a little dated now, because very major companies are really global, in that they regard the whole earth as their marketplace and, although they are officially registered in one 'home' country, they tend to regard the whole world as their home market. This means that they are subject to laws where they are registered but also those in the localities where they have a base.

The influence of the largest multinational companies cannot be exaggerated. They influence many financial and world organizations. Indeed, many are larger in terms of financial turnover than nation states. In recent history, there have been a number of cases where multinational companies have received indirect government support.

The technological ability and organizational scale of these companies means that they often have a significant influence on the private sector organizations in the countries that they work in. They may also have considerable expertise in areas like finance. Sometimes, they will know more about the fiscal affairs of their host country than the government of their host country. The multinational will often have far more legal know-how as well. Of course, such companies will also provide considerable amounts of employment and will often help to develop the local infrastructure. These are desirable attributes, but they also give the multinational considerable influence as well.

Without doubt, multinational companies can generate considerable resources in a third-world country. In some cases, though, the same companies can exploit third-world countries both economically and environmentally. The question that is often asked is this: to what degree can the multinational company take advantage of their host country, perhaps damaging the local environment and exploiting the local workforce? Does the fact that the company has been invited in give them an automatic right to do as they please? Can it be argued, as Friedman no doubt would argue, that the role of the multinational is to make profits and not look after the environment that they are working in? Should the host country simply sit back and be grateful for all the work and currency being brought in?

We have already discussed the question of to what degree should companies use local or home strategies in their treatment of workers. Going international clearly brings in a number of other issues as well. At the end of this chapter is a case study by Harriet Dudley, which looks at the activities of one multinational company, Shell. Before we consider that case, let us look at one other key area of international business ethics – the treatment of bribery and extortion.

Coping with Bribery and Extortion

Bribery is one of the most common ethical problems faced by international managers. Offering bribes is something that many managers resent and yet in some countries it is a condition of doing business. Furthermore in some countries, such as the USA, paying bribes is illegal and can put the manager in a difficult position. On the other hand, resisting bribery can be pointless. If you don't go along with it, you may jeopardize your business while less honest competitors step in.

Are all bribes the same? I would argue not. There is clearly small-scale and large-scale bribery. So-called *Baksheesh* (tips) and grease payments are common in less-developed countries. In some countries, they represent the way that poorly paid government officials supplement their income. It is quite common in some countries to have to pay bribes to officials to gain official papers and so on. In one example I encountered, a businessman went to a country within the former Soviet Union and was told that he needed a visa. He needed it quickly. He was told that this would be possible but a fee would be required. This was duly paid. The 'visa' was then delivered. It had been drawn on a piece of paper in a child's wax crayon! Bemused, the businessman went to the border and gave the 'visa' to the official, who laughed and merrily stamped the visa as being OK.

We might suggest that large-scale bribery aimed at high-level officials is another matter. Bribery of this magnitude is concealed from public view – although these scandals do come to light from time to time. Even in societies where large-scale bribery is more common, the discovery of such activities can result in the unseating of senior people. But does the fact that a practice is widespread mean that it is acceptable?

Bribery can also appear in other areas other than business. Education is a common area for bribery and 'buying' your degree is commonplace in some parts of the world. This really comes back to the 'universal rule' approach, though. If everyone were doing it, would degree certificates mean anything? Clearly not, so why should one person be able to do it?

It should be noted that whilst most business people tend to relate bribery to the developing world, it is by no means uncommon in other parts of the world as well. The form of the bribe may become more subtle – a meal out at a smart restaurant, or some other tangible gift, rather than a brown envelope full of money.

Why Does Bribery Occur Anyway?

Most bribery comes about because of the concept of economic rent. Economic rent occurs when extra revenues are accrued because of a shortage of resources in a given situation. Earlier in the book, I mentioned the high wages of professional footballers, who earn the money that they do because of the relative scarcity of their talents. This extra money is what is known as economic rent. A good deal of bribery is based on this same concept.

The key issues of bribery are best illustrated by looking at some examples. Perhaps the most common examples exist with trade restrictions. Many governments put quotas and import licences on goods flowing into the country. Possession of these licences is highly prized and the issuers of them clearly have considerable power. A good example of this was the so-called licence quota the Raj experienced in India at one time. Almost all goods coming into the country were controlled by import restrictions, and the officials that controlled these had tremendous power. There is some evidence that countries which promote free trade are far less likely to suffer from bribery problems. A related example is where countries issue subsidies for industries. These subsidies should be issued according to government policy and strategy but in reality the picture may be distorted because subsidies may be awarded on the basis of bribes.

As already mentioned, low wages in the public services can also be a major problem. Badly paid officials may be forced to obtain bribes to supplement their incomes. Of course, they are often in a position to do so. For this reason, it may be quite common in some countries to have to pay bribes even to obtain quite simple government services. Rather worryingly, it is not unheard of in some countries for driving licences and even medical degrees to be obtained this way.

There are other factors that might be considered as well. Some countries have multiple exchange rate systems. Essentially, there is one rate for tourists, one for trade, and so on. Of course, defining who is what is not always clear and it may be that the payment of a bribe may result in the most advantageous rate being obtained.

We should distinguish between bribery and extortion. Bribery involves the payment of money or other valuable goods to a public or private official in order to get that official to carry out a certain act. Bribery is usually wrong because these officials should carry out their duties without the need for extra payment. In contrast, extortion usually involves the use of force or coercion to get things done. Blackmail may also be a factor here.

How Do We Deal With Bribery?

Is bribery good for the economies of countries where it is commonplace? Generally, I would suggest that it isn't. Bribery tends to reduce investment into the country. This is because the need to pay bribes to officials inevitably puts off some investors. Most would prefer a level playing field. As a result, the existence of bribery is often held up as a reason for hampering growth in certain economies. Another problem is that it tends to divert the energy of the most able. If it is possible to make a lot of money through bribes, then people with ability will tend to try to get these rather than do a more productive job. Bribery can result in the misallocation of resources.

Many countries have the potential to be rich but they are not because their governments are poor – and they are not very successful at collecting taxes. A friend of mine had a successful business based in a developing country. The taxman came to call. The company had made a profit equivalent to £1 million. The taxman indicated that a large amount of tax would have to be paid. He then indicated that a smaller amount could be paid under 'certain conditions'. These conditions involved paying the taxman £50,000 in used notes. The amount was paid and the taxman wrote in his book that the 'company made a loss'.

Infrastructure and other investment is also affected. (Money that could have been invested is 'creamed off' in the form of bribes.) In addition, there is some evidence that the very composition of government expenditure may be adversely influenced by bribery and extortion. Money may be invested in projects that are not really in the best interests of the country but do suit the aims of the bribers.

Bribery payments are often termed 'grease', which suggests that bribery is used to expedite the process. The bribes are there to smooth out the process. In reality, this is not actually the case. What the bribery is doing of course is simply removing obstacles that have been artificially put in the way by the officials. The more payments that are made, the more obstacles there are that tend to be put up! Would the country not be better off if the obstacles were removed in the first place?

In many countries, the payment of bribes to local officials in order to make things happen is commonplace, particularly amongst small companies. Often, these payments take the form of 'protection' – essentially, if they are not paid, unfortunate things happen to the organization. There is evidence that the cost of these bribes may raise company overheads in some cases by as much as 20 per cent. This really amounts to a substantial local sales tax.

So what do you do? If you have a valuable piece of equipment sitting on some dockside and it is going nowhere until you pay someone, what do you do? What do you tell the stakeholders of the company?

A Possible Solution?

One solution is the following set of rules. The rules suggest that an action – in this case bribery – is acceptable if:

1. The misconduct is publicly acknowledged and is clearly an accepted way of life.
2. Resistance is clearly morally pointless.
3. Resistance is sure to produce more harm than good.

This set of rules errs towards the 'universal' rule view and does have a few problems. Just because 'everyone is doing it', does that mean that it is OK? If everyone in a country was murdering each other and it had become an acceptable way of life – point 1 above – does it mean that it is OK for us to do it? I would suggest not. Rule 2 may give us a different angle. If resisting an action is pointless than perhaps we might wish to go along with it. However, even if it was morally pointless to protest about the level of murder going on – taking the example above – does that mean that it is OK to go and kill people? The third point may well be relevant. If not murdering people would do more harm than good than perhaps we should go on and murder. However, it is very hard to imagine such a situation.

Clearly the rule has its merits but may have its limitations as well from a unitarian point of view. If something is wrong in our country, what suddenly makes it right in another, particularly when it is known that the country in question would probably do better if bribery was irradiated?

The Bhopal Tragedy and the Question of Compensation

The Bhopal disaster was one of the worst events of the 1980s and brought to a light a number of key questions for us to consider. At the time, it was the world's worst industrial accident, although the explosion at Chernobyl proved to be even worse. Let us look at the case and then consider some of the issues involved.

CASE STUDY – **Union Carbide**

Late in the evening of 2 December 1984, a cloud of deadly white gas descended on the shantytown homes of thousands of poor people living on the outskirts of Union Carbide's pesticide plant in the central Indian city of Bhopal. Within hours, at least 2000 people were dead, thousands more lay gasping for breath with seared lungs and burnt eyes and many others faced the prospect of long-term impairment and disease. (More recently, the state government of Madhya Pradesh, in its official documentation of deaths and injuries, reported that approximately 3800 people died, 40 were left with permanent total disability, and 2680 were left with permanent partial disability.)

Despite initial concerns, studies by India's Council of Medical Research indicated that severe injury to the lungs was limited to a small percentage of the population and there was no serious residual eye disease. Union Carbide have since claimed that medical studies have shown that massive, one-time exposure to volatile methyl isocyanate (MIC) has not caused cancer, birth defects, or other delayed manifestations of medical effects.

The Bhopal disaster began innocently enough fifteen years earlier when Union Carbide India Ltd (UCIL), the majority owned subsidiary of the American-based Union Carbide Corporation, established a packaging facility for the pesticide Sevin in Bhopal. The Indian government favoured this step as part of its drive towards alleviating the country's chronic food shortages, while Union Carbide looked forward to securing a foothold in a potentially vast market. In 1978, under an agreement with the government that required it to share technology with its subsidiary, Carbide opened a $25 million Sevin production plant in Bhopal. Modelled on Carbide's US facilities, the plant was designed to produce up to 5000 tons of Sevin per year, using MIC as a basic ingredient.

Events in the early 1980s frustrated Carbide's profit expectations. Economic recession led Indian farmers to seek cheaper alternatives to Sevin, and small-scale producers began to undersell Carbide's product. As early as 1981, the Bhopal plant was losing money; by

1984, management expected a $4 million annual loss. In response, Carbide and UCIL adopted extensive cost-cutting measures. Management cut staff at the MIC facility from twelve to six operators per shift, and reduced the number of maintenance workers. Faulty safety devices went unrepaired for weeks at a time. A refrigerator unit designed for emergency cooling of the three large MIC storage tanks was shut down.

Union Carbide officials were aware of these growing safety and maintenance problems. A 1982 report by a group of Carbide's US engineers itemized the problems, but the parent corporation made little effort to spur the Indian executive responsible for the day-to-day operation of the plant to correct them. The stage was set for disaster.

On 2 December 1984, a large quantity of water was somehow introduced into one of the MIC tanks. Carbide have since claimed that this was a deliberate sabotage by a disgruntled worker and still maintain this in official documents. Others testified that it was an accident made possible by faulty equipment. Whatever the case, a powerful chemical reaction resulted, generating large amounts of heat and pressure. This led to massive, uncontrolled venting of MIC and other poisonous reaction products into the air.

Analysis

The Bhopal disaster resulted in a difficult legal case. Was the US parent responsible for compensation, or the UCIL? The former had net assets of $10 billion, while UCIL was worth $250 million. Should damages be pegged at the same level of survivors of other similar disasters in India or should they be at US levels?

In 1989, the supreme Court of India made Carbide pay compensation of $470 million. On 24 February of that year both UCIL and Carbide agreed to this. The payments have been paid very slowly, although interest has been added to the decreed amount. As a result of this, the total amount paid out is more like $1 billion. By December 1994, Carbide fulfilled its commitment for a Bhopal hospital, with about $20 million being turned over to the charitable trust. An additional $54 million from the sale of Carbide shares in UCIL went to the hospital and local clinics. Groundbreaking for the hospital began in mid-October 1995 and, according to Indian press reports, the hospital was expected to be operational in early 2000.

Pause for thought ...
How responsible would you say Union Carbide were in this case? They firmly maintain that the plant was sabotaged, and there appears no concrete proof to the contrary. However, there was clear evidence that they knew that there were safety problems at the plant and there are clear signs of cost cutting here.

The compensation issue is also interesting. Had the disaster happened in California, Carbide would have been liquidated to pay compensation. As it was, the payment, though substantial, was relatively small, although appreciable by Indian standards. This brings forward another key question. What price a life? Can we justify paying out far less money to an Indian than an American because Indians earn less? What criteria should we use? Would Union Carbide have been so careless with their safety precautions if they had been threatened with such a large compensation bill?

The International Manager's Responsibilities

The international manager has a difficult task from an ethical point of view. Not only does he or she have to deal with their own ethical standards, they also have to take into account the values of others. On the one hand, it can be argued that we have no moral right whatsoever to tell people from one country how to deal with a situation. They have their culture and we should respect this. However, how far should this go?

The following case study by Harriet Dudley looks at the operations of a major international company in an overseas situation. You should read it through whilst thinking about the above questions.

Case Study – Shell International: True Torchbearers?

(*By Harriet Dudley*)

Ethical Background to the Case

Shell International, which is owned by Royal Dutch/Shell and which encompasses all of the Shell trading companies including Shell USA and Shell Nigeria or Shell Petroleum Development Company (SPDC) as it is now known, has invested billions of dollars in what it terms 'sustainable development' business practices. The purpose of this case study is to examine whether Shell International (referred to on occasion as 'Shell') has truly transformed its business practices to become more 'ethical', or if its massive investment was merely a 'greenwash' or a public-relations exercise. In order to assess this, it is first important to define what are meant by 'ethical' business practices.

In dictating what is morally 'right', ethics form the foundations of all law, government and religion, and therefore guide the behaviour of citizens within their societies. Companies, like any other type of organization, have established their own ethical codes of conduct (whether formal or informal) based on a combination of legal requirements (such as respecting employee rights) and business strategies to further their organizational goals. There has long been a school of thought that companies should do more for society than simply obey its laws, that they should reinvest in local communities some of what they gain in profit from making use of society's environment and inhabitants. (In other words, how much a company gives back to society, in addition to its legal or business requirements.) The World Business Council on Sustainable Development (WBCSD), a coalition of 120 international companies committed to the principles of economic growth and sustainable development), sees the issues at the forefront of the debate on 'corporate social responsibility' as being 'human rights, employee rights, environmental protection, supplier relations and community involvement'. (WBCSD, 'Meeting Changing Expectations: Corporate Social Responsibility', at page 3.) It suggests that all of these must be addressed in any corporate code of practice.

Their shareholders own all companies, and therefore all employees of the company are duty bound to act in whichever way will benefit their shareholders most. The traditional view is that shareholders want their companies to be as valuable as possible (as measured by the price or value allocated to individual shares of the company). One of the ways in which shares are valued is according to the amount of profit the company makes, and so managers tend to prioritize profit as their main criterion for decision-making. A fundamental principle of ethical decision-making is to change that priority and replace the needs of the shareholder with those of the stakeholder.

A stakeholder is anyone who will be affected by the decision and so can include parties exterior to the organization. Stakeholders can be separated into two bodies of people: those who are essential to the existence and prosperity of the organization (stockholders, employees, suppliers, and the local community that provides facilities and/or employees); and any group or individual that can indirectly be affected by the organization (for example, even non-car drivers are affected by car manufacturers when they breathe exhaust fumes). It has been argued that because stakeholders such as employees and groups of local citizens are vital to the success of the company, their interests must be reconciled with those of the shareholder in managerial decision-making. The stakeholder theory of the firm takes the view that the role of the manager is as arbiter in negotiating business codes of conduct between different stakeholder groups, while ensuring the survival of the firm. Structures could be established such as a stakeholder advisory board and a stakeholder bill of rights, both of which would give stakeholders some form of representation at corporate level.

As stakeholders, the welfare of local people and the local environment should be of concern to an ethical organization, and it should try to minimize any harmful effects it may have, directly or indirectly, upon them. It could employ 'cradle-to-grave' policies that track company procedures from the input to the output, from start to finish. As has been seen by disasters such as the Bhopal gas leak in 1984, which killed at least 3000 local people, or the more recent oil spill off the coast of Brittany, companies often sacrifice health and safety measures in their drive for profit.

Although there is some environmental control by legislation (the UK has laws to protect the quality of water and air), most decisions concerning the manufacture and distribution of a product are left to the discretion of companies themselves. Governments are often unwilling to draw up environmental legislation for fear of losing the generous contributions made to their political parties by polluting companies. There are also many difficulties in enforcing existing environmental legislation, for example establishing the effected parties can be complex, and penalties are difficult to legislate because environmental damage cannot easily be costed.

Capitalism, and the protection of property such as shares by governmental legislation, has presented companies with a conflict of interest when it comes to environmental protection. They understandably ask themselves 'If it is not profitable to be green why should we bother?'. This reduces trees and clean air to commodities to be chosen or discarded according to their worth, in the marketplace. Unfortunately, we discard them at our peril, as has been shown by the severe environmental degradation caused by greenhouse gases and their consequent changes to weather patterns. The result is that society often pays the 'external' costs, those not covered by the company, of cleaning up, or simply enduring, the waste it produces. Nevertheless, the neglectful and often reckless behaviour shown by companies over recent years is changing. Increasingly companies such as Union Carbide, which paid out millions of dollars in compensation to the Bhopal victims, are considering investments in health and safety and environmental protection as necessary costs. Few companies can afford such huge payouts when accidents do happen.

An integral part of business ethics and stakeholder theory is the protection of human rights. These are laid out in the United Nations Universal Declaration on Human Rights, which declares that all humans have a right to such essentials as food, clothing and shelter. Codes of conduct as adopted by companies usually insist on basic standards of worker's rights such as prohibiting child and forced labour, banning discrimination based on race, religion or ethnic origin and limiting working hours and forced overtime. These types of guidelines are particularly necessary for multinational organizations. Technological advances have furthered the globalization of capitalism, enabling companies to shift production facilities to countries where costs are low and where labour and environmental standards either do not exist or are minimal. The use of 'sweatshops' where employees work long hours, often in cramped conditions, for meagre wages, is still favoured by many large manufacturing companies, both in developed and developing countries.

As described so far, ethical codes of conduct would not seem to be too difficult for companies to employ. However, managers of multinational firms often find it difficult to adapt to the culture of a host country while implementing the code of conduct established by head office. Companies are often accused of being 'ethical chameleons', of changing their codes of practice to take advantage of the environment they are in (e.g. a company may not provide the same benefits for employees working in host countries as they do for those in head office). Bluffing and bribing are just two examples of what many companies would call standard business practices, but which could have a negative impact on the local community by encouraging dishonesty and the corrupt practices of government officials. One of the first lessons for an international MBA student is the importance, as a multinational, of being 'multi-local', able to adapt standard business practices to respect the local culture, religion and traditions. So it is easy to see how many managers believe they are doing the right thing by adopting a 'when in Rome' approach to their activities.

A History of Shell in Nigeria

Shell International is a multinational company that is in both the downstream and upstream sectors of the oil and gas industry. It has subsidiaries in many countries, Shell Nigeria/SPDC being one of its most troublesome, with a turbulent history spanning the last 30 years. Shell International has suffered many years of negative publicity caused by incidents such as the Brent Spar debacle (1991–5) when the company fought to be allowed to dump one of its oil-storage buoys into the Atlantic Ocean. There was also the fire in which hundreds of Nigerians perished (17 October 1998) caused by a pipeline leaking oil which highlighted the lack of health and safety precautions by oil companies in the region, and the highly publicized (continuing) struggle of the Ogoni people. The company has been the subject of world-wide consumer boycotts and has suffered the disruption of its activities, the destruction of its oilrigs and other property, and an ensuing fall in its share price. As a result, Shell International has recently invested billions of dollars in an attempt to persuade the public that its priorities have changed and that along with its subsidiary SPDC, it has become, amongst other things, a 'better corporate citizen in Nigeria'. ('The Shell Report 1999: People, Planet & Profits', cover note.) It has reinvented itself as a company that lives by the principles of sustainable development that 'meets the needs of the present without compromising the ability of future generations to meet their own needs'. This contrasts strongly with Shell Nigeria's past corporate code of conduct.

Oil was first struck in the Niger Delta region in 1956 and the local people celebrated, thinking their lives were about to be transformed. They were right, but not in the way they had imagined. In fact, the people of the region have never benefited from the millions of dollars' worth of oil that makes up 90 per cent of their country's total export and 80 per cent of their government's revenue. Instead, they have suffered environmental destruction of their habitat on a massive scale. The Ogoni people are one of a number of groups of impoverished peoples living in the oil-rich area of the Niger Delta. For at least 30 years the Ogoni people have been fighting, through their pressure group, the Movement for the Survival of Ogoni People (MOSOP), for the right to protect and control their land and also for a share in the profit it produces. Until recently, SPDC and the Nigerian government had never consulted MOSOP over actions taken involving their land, or reinvested any of the profit produced by the company into the local community.

The anger and frustration came to a head in 1995 when General Sani Abacha, the military dictator of Nigeria at the time, hanged Ken Saro Wiwa, environmentalist and leader of the MOSOP movement, along with nine other Ogoni activists. This action shocked the world, and led to Commonwealth sanctions being imposed against Nigeria (which have only recently been removed), but it also demonstrated the determination of the Nigerian government to protect the interests of their corporate guests. Indeed, the recent revelation that Abacha's family stole $4 billion during his regime goes some way towards explaining the aggressive behaviour exhibited by the dictator, and shows where the oil money really went.

Shell Nigeria/SPDC has been accused on many occasions of working alongside the Nigerian government in its attempts to suppress the non-violent protests of the MOSOP campaigners. According to Essential

Action, an organization that still encourages the boycotting of Shell International, both Shell and the Nigerian government have admitted that Shell contributed to the funding of the military regime in the Delta region (taken from Essential Action's website). It claims that Shell has twice admitted paying the military to go to specific villages in order to suppress the peaceful demonstrations of the Ogoni residents by destroying houses and vital crops. Far more sinister is the fact that Shell Nigeria was also implicated in the killing in 1990 of 80 people in the village of Umeuchem, close to Ogoniland. According to Glenn Ellis, director of the film *The Drilling Fields* (1994, Catma Films), each of the military missions paid for by Shell Nigeria resulted in Ogoni fatalities. The MOSOP website is as damning of Shell as Essential Action is. It speaks of 'shootings, rapes, arbitrary arrests, mass looting, extortion, torture and imprisonment in degrading conditions at the hands of a military that is armed by and paid for by the Shell oil company'. As a result of state-orchestrated violence, it claims that over 2000 Ogoni have died and approximately 30,000 have been forced to leave their homes. What is certain is that, as a result of the disturbances, since 1994 the military have been a permanent presence in the once-peaceful Ogoniland. When the new democratic leadership came into power under the leadership of President Obasanjo, it set up a commission to look into human-rights abuses by former military governments. The commission was overwhelmed with submissions; the majority of them, around 8000, came from MOSOP.

The suffering of the Ogoni people continued when, as has already been mentioned, on 17 October 1998, over 700 people were burnt alive and hundreds more were seriously burnt when oil spilling from a pipeline caught alight. The local people had come to collect the gushing oil, which is such a rare commodity these days in Nigeria. Although it is not clear which oil company owned the pipeline, Shell Nigeria has routinely placed oil pipelines above ground in the region. By contrast, the majority of Shell pipelines in the USA and Western Europe are placed below ground, a safety precaution that would have prevented the tragedy in Nigeria. Local hospital facilities, including those to which Shell had contributed financially, were too few and too ill equipped to be able to deal with the casualties, and victims were left untreated for days. A sign of the mistrust felt by most Nigerians for the government was the growth of the death toll in the weeks that followed the fire, as victims who had been afraid of seeking treatment for fear of being arrested died from their injuries. Relatives removed their loved ones from hospital prematurely for the same reason. The Nigerian government offered to pay the medical bills, but refused compensation on the grounds that the leak was caused by vandalism.

It is important to note that the government and most officialdom in Nigerian society have an established practice of bribing and accepting bribes in order to achieve most day-to-day activities. Police routinely, and for no official reason, stop cars and ask for a 'dash' (the local word for a bribe, seen more as a tip) and even passport controllers at Lagos airport expect this type of payment for simply doing their job. In an environment such as this, Shell Nigeria/SPDC would undoubtedly have found it difficult to function without either obliging requests for payments or taking an anti-bribery stance and thereby risking the non-cooperation of local officials. It would also be difficult to establish how much of what Shell Nigeria/SPDC paid would have been for the protection of their staff and property, in other words the basic duties of local police, and how much would have been paid for illegal services such as those mentioned above. If there is such a thing as a 'compensation culture' in the region that now leads the local people to demand a share of the profits, it is in part the result of Shell International's practice of paying off local chiefs or leaders when oil spills have taken place. It could be argued that by owning a subsidiary in a 'corrupt' country like Nigeria, Shell International has the perfect excuse for behaving like an ethical chameleon.

Protests by MOSOP and other campaigners, who have seen little advancement of their cause through peaceful demonstrations, have become increasingly violent in recent years and the operations of Shell Nigeria/SPDC have been disrupted by protests in the Delta region. In October 1998, Shell International issued a press release saying it could no longer guarantee supplies of crude oil from Nigeria after armed protesters seized more than ten stations, two helicopters and a drilling rig. By the end of that year, Ijaw activists had shut down twenty pumping stations, halving onshore output for two months; the action halted more than a fifth of the country's oil output of two million barrels-per-day. According to a BBC report, the Ijaw tribe, who were demanding self-government and that all oil companies leave the area, caused the damage (taken from a BBC website). The activists claim that it is the government they are targeting through companies like Shell, knowing how strongly their government officials depend on the income from oil companies. In February 1999, different groups and tribes from the region gathered in Port Harcourt for their first-ever meeting. Although there were the inevitable disputes, they were unanimous about several things: all of them were suffering from polluted rivers, disrupted farming and cut-down forests and had received no benefit in compensation from oil-related activities.

Shell has long been accused, by international development and environmental agencies, of neglecting the Ogoni people. Ogoni villages have no clean water, little electricity and no jobs for farmers and fishermen displaced by the oil companies. Over the years the oil company has only ever employed 88 Ogoni people, only 2 per cent of Shell's employees in Nigeria. ('Black Gold, White Heat' by Michael Watts in *Geographies of Resistance* (ed. Steven Pile, Keith Michael).) The Nigerian Environmental Study Action Team has observed that there has been an increase in certain diseases in the region, such as bronchial asthma, gastro-enteritis and cancer, as a result of the oil industry. There is also a substantial amount of acid rain that falls in the area due to the frequent oil fires when attempts are made to burn off oil spills.

Ken Saro Wiwa called the process of natural gas flaring 'the most notorious action' of Shell and other oil companies. In Ogoniland, 95 per cent of natural gases are flared, compared to 0.6 per cent in the USA. Consequently, it is estimated that Nigerian oil fields are responsible for more global warming effects than the combined oil fields of the rest of the world. In addition, the Ogoni people have witnessed countless oil leaks so that their rivers are polluted and their land is virtually smothered in highly destructive crude oil. Between 1976 and 1991 there were 2976 oil spills in the Delta region. Even though Nigeria only accounts for 14 per cent of Shell's production, 40 per cent of the company's oil spills have occurred there. Shell's high-pressure pipelines were constructed above ground, through villages and criss-cross over land that was once used for agricultural purposes, rendering it economically useless. Many pipelines pass within metres of Ogoni homes. Because of nearly four decades of oil extraction, the Niger Delta, home to coastal rainforest and mangrove habitats, is the most endangered river delta in the world.

In a UN Special Rapporteur's report on Nigeria published in April 1998, the UN accused Shell and the Nigerian Government of abusing human rights and failing to protect the environment in oil-producing regions, and called for an investigation into Shell. A second report, released in November of the same year, made the same accusations, and condemned Shell for its 'well-armed security force, which is intermittently employed against protesters'. Nigeria's membership of the Commonwealth was suspended in 1995 after the execution of Ken Saro Wiwa. MOSOP is against the Commonwealth minister's recommendation to readmit Nigeria now that there is a new civilian government, claiming that nothing has been done to address the fundamental grievances of the Ogoni people.

However the USA, as the loudest supporter of human rights but also the largest consumer of Nigerian oil, didn't taken any action to show its disapproval of the Nigerian non-democratic system. Instead, it put into place legislation to prevent individual US states boycotting Nigerian exports, warning them that such action would jeopardize US membership of the World Trade Organization. Shell US has, in the past, tried to distance itself from the activities of Shell Nigeria/SPDC. But both Shell US and Shell Nigeria/SPDC have the same parent company, Shell International, and nearly half of Nigerian oil export is distributed in the USA.

Shell's Transformation into a Socially Responsible Business Leader

Shell has embarked on a costly public involvement exercise, which included CD-ROMs for schools and journalists and 'stakeholder' dialogue sessions for environmentalists around Europe. It has participated in projects organized by the WBCSD, including a publication entitled 'Meeting Changing Expectations: Corporate Social Responsibility', which has been mentioned above. This document sets forth standards and makes practical suggestions as to how companies should implement ethical practices, while reminding them of the benefits of giving something back to society. (Shell International is among other companies such as Rio Tinto, Unilever and General Motors that have contributed examples of their own initiatives.) Shell refers to the publication of its introductory guide for managers on human rights, which forms part of an 'awareness program designed to help managers deal with the issue in their work'. It also refers to its human-rights website, launched in 1998, which forms part of its Intranet and as such is available to Shell managers worldwide.

The Shell Report 1999 entitled 'People, Planet & Profits: an Act of Commitment', which has been mentioned above, is a 44-page glossy document with an introduction by Shell's Chairman of the Committee of Managing Directors, Mark Moody-Stuart. Here he insists that Shell's 'values, business principles, commitment to contribute to a sustainable form of development – and the candid reporting of our performance in those areas – are inextricably linked to our long-term commercial success'. The Shell Statement of General Business Principles, which consists of nine fundamental principles that the company tries to live by, is printed on the back cover of the document. These principles serve to refute accusations made by Essential Action and the UN, namely that Shell has worked alongside the Nigerian government and has admitted to, on occasion, bribing them. Under Principle 5 entitled 'Political Activities' it claims: 'Shell companies do not make payments to political parties, organisations or their representatives.' It continues under 'Business Integrity': 'the direct or indirect offer, payment, soliciting and acceptance of bribes in any form are unacceptable practices'.

Shell condemns what it calls the 'double standards' of some multinational organizations, insisting their 'environmental management policy applies globally. We have minimum standards on which all Shell companies worldwide are expected to improve'. It makes many promises and guarantees OECD standard environmental protective practices. However when referring to potential hazards such as oil spills, it chooses its words carefully, saying only that 'national laws on clean-up differ but in most cases it is up to the company to identify contamination and take the appropriate action, if any is needed'. This seems to contradict its earlier statement, implying that Shell's actions depend on local legislation, and not company policy. In addition it points out that 'contaminated soil can be harmful but it is often harmless unless the contaminant is seeping in to surrounding areas ... we have adopted a recognised risk assessment method to find out whether contaminants pose a threat to health or the environment', the implication being that if it doesn't, then the contamination is left untreated.

The environment section of the report refers to its practice of disposing of gas that is produced as a by-product of oil production, by flaring. It claims that its new US$ 3.8 million liquefied natural gas plant in Nigeria will change this by allowing the company to sell gas that was previously flared. Shell plans to expand the plant while increasing Nigeria's oil production, and claims to be committed to ending gas flaring entirely by 2008.

Further on in the document there is an area devoted to human rights, which includes a paragraph entitled 'Nigeria Update' where it admits 'progress towards reconciliation has been slow'. It claims that SPDC 'does not use force or seek armed intervention to suppress demonstrations by communities protesting peacefully, even if it disrupts production'. It has organized three stakeholder meetings with community representatives, local and foreign non-governmental organizations and government agencies. One of the most recent, in October 1998, discussed SPDC's social investment policy and its transition from assistance to development.

As a part of its 1998 Annual Report, Shell Nigeria/SPDC included a lengthy section entitled Community Report, which laid out developments the organization had made during the year towards its goal of sustainable development. SPDC community spending increased by 37 per cent to US$43 million in 1998. It refers to a new Community Programme Development Department that was established in 1997 and which, in 1998 recruited 25 Nigerian professionals in areas such as health care, agriculture, education and water and sanitation.

Shell has contributed and sponsored many other publications that take the theme of corporate social responsibility. In a *Financial Times* supplement entitled 'Responsible Business', Shell's logo on the front cover indicates that the company has sponsored the publication. It includes a large double-page advertisement that outlines the company's commitment to human rights, and an article written by Shell chairman Mark Moody-Stuart on the subject of Shell's environmental commitments. Here, the chairman claims that Shell has already met the requirements set during the Kyoto summit of 1997 for all industrialized countries (i.e. to reduce greenhouse gas emissions by at least 5.2 per cent by 2008), although it doesn't say by how much it has exceeded the target. Shell is also investing US$500 million over five years (1999–2004) in improving its skills in areas such as solar power, forestry and biomass energy. This is as a result of the company's prediction that renewable energy sources could gain 50 per cent of the energy market by 2050.

However, Mr Moody-Stuart continues, ambiguously, 'countries will choose different policies to meet Kyoto targets, including ... emission permit trading, and Shell will consider these when making its investment decisions'. Shell knows that fossil fuels will still be the main energy requirement for the next 20–30 years, largely as a result of emission permit trading which allows companies to maintain its current carbon-dioxide emission levels by paying other, economically weaker, neighbouring countries to shoulder the burden. This has already been done by Japan, which is paying Australia to grow forests, which will soak up the Japanese emissions that exceed the Kyoto target. This practice has been criticized by environmentalists as being inefficient because as soon as the trees are cut or fall down, the CO^2 is released back into the atmosphere.

Shell is a member of the Prince of Wales Business Leader's Forum (PWBF) and is credited by the Forum with playing a leadership role in formulating the International Chamber of Commerce's Business Charter for Sustainable Development. The PWBF website praises Shell for acknowledging 'that its responsibility towards society is to conduct business as responsible corporate members of society'.

In 1997 Shell formed its Social Accountability team. At that time, the company contacted SustainAbility Ltd, a consultancy and lobbyist for corporate social responsibility initiatives which had been critics of Shell International in the past, and were a little sceptical when asked by the company to help guide it towards a more sustainable and accountable approach to business. Like many of Shell's stakeholders, critics and the general public, SustainAbility 'had significant concerns that Shell's approach ... was simply part of a crisis-driven public-relations exercise' (see their website). However, they worked with Shell for two years, having set them the challenge of becoming 'the leading multi-national in economic, environmental and social responsibility' and published a report on their assessment of the effectiveness of the relationship on their website. The recommendations made by SustainAbility were generally adopted by Shell via its Social Accountability team (now the Shell Sustainable Development Group) who were 'consistently receptive to the challenges'.

According to SustainAbility, Shell has succeeded in demonstrating that awareness has changed both in the markets in which Shell operates and in the company itself. Shell has demonstrated a 'very strong commitment to feedback through reports, Shell's website and stakeholder engagement'. The company's withdrawal from the Global Climate Coalition (a powerful lobbying group made up of representatives from mainly US oil companies that has succeeded in preventing the US Congress from adopting any of the recommendations from the Kyoto summit on CO_2 reduction) was welcomed by SustainAbility, although it comments that 'the issues posed by memberships of other industry and lobbying groups could be more clearly identified and addressed'. Finally, when Shell was set the challenge to help define industry or sector benchmarks, SustainAbility credits the company with becoming 'something of a leader and a benchmark company not only in the oil industry but more generally'.

In order to assess this praise, we should compare the commitment to sustainable development that has been made by Shell International with that made by other oil companies. Exxon/Mobil, for example, has been far less committal and admits that its priority has been simply to stay within the law. It makes no mention of social responsibility on its website, or any commitment to investigating alternatives to fossil fuels. The closest competition for Shell in its drive to be the most popular player in the oil and gas industry is BP Amoco. This company has been investing in solar power for years, through its subsidiary BP Solarex, the largest solar-power company in the world. According to Rodney Chase, deputy chief executive officer of BP Amoco, solar power is 'not just for the future but for the present' (speech at the Franco-British Chamber of Commerce and Industry, Paris, 2 July 1999), which is why the multinational has begun a global programme to install solar panels on their retail sites. They have also made a commitment to bring 'clean fuels' (ultra-low sulphur diesel) into 40 cities around the world during 1999 and 2000. They have started to reduce their greenhouse gas emissions and are working towards eliminating natural gas flaring (although unlike Shell, no time frame is given).

BP Amoco has adopted a Policy Commitment to Health, Safety and Environment Performance and a Policy Commitment to Ethical Conduct, which follows the UN Declaration's principles. It claims to adhere to the OECD guidelines, the International Labour Organization Declaration of Principles Concerning Multinational Enterprises and Social Policy and Amnesty International's Human Rights Guidelines for Companies. However, few examples of practical changes made within the multinational or externally, through its stakeholders, are given to support these commitments. Unlike Shell, BP Amoco has not invited an external consultancy such as SustainAbility to measure its progress, and doesn't allow itself to be accountable to its stakeholders via its website.

In addition, BP Amoco has been criticized by agencies such as Oxfam, Save the Children and Amnesty International for its conduct in several war-torn countries. In Casanare, Columbia, the company is accused of not ensuring that its social responsibility policies are given as much importance at a local level as they are at head office. In order to protect its $2 billion investment in the region, its staff and production facilities, from the violence caused by civil war, the company has relied heavily on local police and the military who stand accused of human-rights abuses. In a situation similar to that of Shell in Nigeria, relations between BP Amoco and the local people have deteriorated in recent months, with accusations that the company was complicit in the murders of local activists opposed to its operations. However, unlike Shell, BP Amoco hasn't invested in establishing relations with local non-governmental organizations, trying to reinvest in the community and begin reconciliation. BP Amoco has also invested heavily in Sudan, where the fundamentalist regime is accused of carrying out genocide financed by the country's oil revenue. The company has a $570 million stake in PetroChina which is helping to build a new pipeline that will more than double Sudan's production, spreading the oil war far beyond its present borders. BP Amoco has rejected appeals by non-governmental organizations to end its investment in the area, insisting it will increase its stake in PetroChina to $1 billion, provoking the response by Amnesty International that: 'In buying into PetroChina, BP is investing in oil in Sudan and has to take responsibility for human-rights abuses in the area' (Britain backs ugly war for oil' by J. Flint in *Observer*, 16 April 2000).

Shell has invested heavily in attempts at reconciliation with the local people in the Niger Delta region. SPDC has increased its budget by 37 per cent and has organized regular meetings with community representatives in order to assess stakeholder needs. However there is some evidence that this is not enough. On 14 April 2000, military police are believed to have killed five people and arrested Ledum Mitee, head of MOSOP, following resistance by local people to Shell building a ten-mile road as part of its programme of reconciliation. According to an article in the *Guardian* newspaper, MOSOP and some communities had complained that there was 'little consultation and that it was not a development priority' (I. Vidal, 'Violence returns to Niger Delta', *Guardian*, 15 April 2000).

Similar accusations have been made over Shell's investments in hospital facilities in the area. The Gokana hospital, built as part of Shell's 1996 Ogoni Reconciliation plan, is an example of how easy it is to squander resources if there has been an inadequate assessment of needs beforehand. There, the new water tower looks good but it doesn't work and there is no money to run the generator on which it depends. The hospital staff claims it would have been far cheaper to restore the old tank, which would have benefited hundreds of people in the nearby village. Shell has contributed a new sterilizing machine, which has been left unopened because 'there is no money to pay people to install it, no electricity to power it and no one knows how to use it' (I. Vidal, 'Oil wealth buys health in country within a country', *Guardian*, 16 September 1999). The local people claim that no one was consulted and no Shell representative has ever visited Gokana. Therefore Shell needs to improve its relations with non-governmental organizations in the area in order to assess properly how best its investments in the local community can be made, so that its attempts at reconciliation do not do more harm than good.

Conclusion

Shell International has made significant progress towards becoming 'a better corporate citizen in Nigeria', even if it had little choice but to radically modify its public-relations strategy following a world-wide boycott and dramatic fall in its share price in the 1980s. It has not been deterred by what Will Day, chief executive of Care International UK, refers to as 'sceptical audiences, both amongst the business financial community, which may see profitability and shareholder value as paramount, and within a development sector more used to seeing companies as part of the problem than the solution' (Shell Report 1999, p. 27). It has established a corporate code of practice, which it tries to enforce throughout the organization using tools such as its human rights website, which is accessible by Shell managers world-wide. Its chairman and top management have participated publicly in the sustainable development debate and contributed their time as well as financial resources to a number of meetings, lectures and publications on the subject.

In an attempt to prevent accusations that it is only interested in 'greenwash', and as proof of its commitment to accountability, Shell invited a previously hostile consultancy to aid and assess its transformation, which has contributed to the benchmarking process of this relatively new movement. As a result it has gained considerable respect from sustainable development advocates such as WBCSD, PWBLF and SustainAbility and Shell chief executive officer Mark Moody-Stuart won the 1999 TOMORROW Environmental Leadership Award for 'setting Shell on a course towards sustainable development and thus spearheading an historic shift in corporate thinking' (*Tomorrow* magazine, Sept./Oct. 1999, p. 12). In this context, they could be argued to be torchbearers for the movement towards corporate social responsibility.

However, although Shell cannot be held responsible for the actions of the Nigerian government, it has undoubtedly been the cause of much of the violence against the people of the Niger Delta region in the past and, to an extent, has profited from it. Accusations of collaborations between Shell and the Nigerian government in the suppression of protests and peaceful demonstrations remain, and recent attacks on Shell property in the region are a reflection of the continued anger of the local people towards the multinational. MOSOP still urges the boycott of Shell products and its members, claiming that little has changed for the better in the Niger Delta region. Shell may have improved its employment policies, but it has created few actual jobs for local people. It has made commitments to reducing its greenhouse emissions, ending gas flaring and investing in alternatives to fossil fuels. However, alongside these commitments, it should be doing more to clean up its oil spills in the Delta region and reversing some of the environmental damage it has already caused. It would seem that the majority of changes that have taken place following Shell's decision to become a 'better corporate citizen in Nigeria' have been internal. They have taken place in the philosophy of the chief executive officer and his management team, whose commitment has been proven by the allocation of significant financial resources that have not, as yet, been transformed into benefits for the stakeholders for whom they are intended.

CHAPTER 10

Corporate Responsibility and the Future of Business Ethics

The 1990s saw an increasing move towards corporate responsibility. The reasons for this have been alluded to throughout this book and include:

1. *The development of communication.* The power of technology cannot be exaggerated. Two facts are often cited. First, that the computing power used in each Saturn 5 rocket that went to the moon was less than that in a modern Ford Escort. The idea of the astronauts 'going to the moon in a family car' is a frightening concept, but certainly as far as computing power was concerned this was the case. An even more startling fact is that the computing power of the music player in a musical birthday card is greater than all of the computing power used by the allies in the Second World War! Today's citizen has computing and communication power that could not have been dreamt of only a few years ago. The implications of this are tremendous. People now have access to information – not all of it accurate – that would not have been available to them only a few years ago. It is worth noting that the very *availability* of the Internet will have a great impact on business ethics. Today it is far less likely that 'secrets' can be kept. What is more, if a secret does come along, the would-be whistleblower can find any number of websites detailing how they might deal with the situation. People who had previously no information about the

outside world can obtain it. Some countries, mindful of this, are trying to prevent them seeing everything they might.

2. *The 'new work paradigm'*. In recent times we have seen a sea change from economies primarily based on manufacturing to economies based on services. We have also seen a very different set of attitudes towards careers. In the past, most people thought in terms of having one career and very often planned to stay with one company for the rest of their lives. This led to considerable loyalty. 'You look after us and we will look after you.' You kept your mouth shut and your hands clean and at the end of the day collected your gold watch and quietly retired. This work pattern is rapidly disappearing. The growth of outsourcing (obtaining services from people outside the organization) is one aspect of this. The implication is that the corporation has less control over many of the people producing goods and services. What is more, the outsourcers will have limited or no loyalty to the organization – after all they work for themselves – and even the full-time employees may have a different view. If a job is no longer for life, loyalty may be less important. We have seen from some of the cases from the past such as the Manville and the Ford Pinto cases that loyalty seemed to play a part. This may not apply so much in the future. Essentially, the cultural cohesiveness of the workplace has been weakened. We can no longer simply assume that most of the workers and managers who come into the workplace have a common set of values.
3. *The structure of organizations*. We have seen the flattening of traditional, hierarchical pyramids. A result of this is that the power of middle management has reduced. These changes have tended to open up accountability and responsibility because no longer can the people at the top be 'protected from what is going on below'. The argument that 'we did not know what was going on' also seems less tenable as well. We might note that the change in the shape of pyramids is partly the result of the new technology such as email and Intranets, which have greatly sped up information dissemination in the modern office.
4. *Globalization*. The early cases in this book generally occurred in times where the only real source of competition was the West. The last few decades have seen a considerable upsurge from the Far East, Japan in particular. The success of these countries has posed a number of questions to Western managers. Traditional management styles have been based on conflict, been short term and rather 'macho' in their approach. Japanese management, with its emphasis

on team building, cooperation and long termism, has certainly made Western management think.

5. *Popular disenchantment with the standards set by business and political leaders.* At one time, business managers and owners were regarded as 'gentlemen' and were above reproach. Similar comments could be made about politicians and leaders generally. The increased education of people generally has created a certain level of cynicism about the whole culture of authority. People are far more likely to question the actions of their leaders now. This may present some problems, but it also does make it far less likely that leaders will get away with major indiscretions without question.

Many of the cases that we have discussed in this book occurred in the 1980s. This is an interesting observation because, in fact, the 1980s were relatively unimportant for corporate responsibility. Much of this can be explained by the fact that when economic growth and material values are the main aims in life, morality tends to take a back seat. However, a range of events, including the *Herald of Free Enterprise* tragedy and the Bhopal disaster, began to make people think more.

Initially, most people saw these cases as being examples of breaches in company safety performance and a lack of working to the rules. This is certainly the case with the *Herald of Free Enterprise* case, to be discussed shortly. However, there began to be questions about the wider issues involved. Above all, was it just the people on the ground that were to blame – or the organization as a whole?

Invariably these disasters cost the company involved a fortune. According to one estimate, over 60 per cent of industrial sites where these disasters occur cease operating afterwards. A good example is that of the *Exxon Valdez*. A large oil tanker, owned by the global oil company Exxon, ran aground in Alaska. It was later found that the captain was drunk at the time. The company spent $2 billion clearing up the damage after the oil spill in addition to making payments totalling $1.1 billion to the US and Alaskan authorities. Even a company the size of Exxon cannot take financial damage like this lightly. Increasingly, companies are looking at safety issues from a cost-benefit point of view, if not from a moral point of view. The question has to be asked, can companies afford not to make safety provision?

The Role of Company Directors

What are the responsibilities of the directors to the stakeholders of the business? We have already considered the stakeholder issue a little earlier in the book. Should directors only be concerned with the shareholders of the company or should they have a wider responsibility to consider? If so, how do these responsibilities affect the way they work? How should they prioritize their responsibilities? Is one stakeholder more important than another? If so, why?

When can directors (and therefore the company) be held responsible for offences committed by junior personnel who have broken company rules but have not been properly selected, trained, instructed or supervised? Obviously there are limits as to how much a board of directors can be made responsible for individual acts, but they cannot wash their hands of everything that happened.

How much should people at the top of the organization know about that company's day-to-day operations? Technology is certainly improving and communications are far better than they were. In this day and age, can a director use the excuse of ignorance, especially if they have failed to set up and maintain effective operating systems in the first place? If they claim that they have not heard about something, might it be their fault for not setting up systems to ensure that they did hear?

Should directors be qualified, educated people? This sounds like a strange question perhaps, but the fact is that in most cases a person does not need any specific qualifications or experience to become a director. Very often, if they commit unethical acts, they may well be prevented from being a director for some time, but essentially any adult citizen can become a company director, irrespective of their background. The idea of having a 'director's entrance exam' is perhaps fanciful, but I think that we can suggest that a more responsible attitude to appointment might be appropriate.

Directors react differently to disasters. In the case of the *Herald of Free Enterprise*, the chairman of the ferry company, Jeffery Sterling, put all the blame on the three men directly involved, and felt that it was 'a bit far-fetched to expect someone on shore to be blamed'. While when a Japan airlines Boeing 747 crashed in 1985, killing 250 people, the company's president resigned.

> Pause for thought ... Should the head of a large company resign when a disaster of this nature occurs, even if he or she had no direct influence over the event in question?

Can the law help? We have seen throughout this book that one major problem is that the law tends to operate on the heels of ethics rather than in advance of it. Generally, the law follows morality rather than the other way around. We can certainly say that the law relating to corporate responsibility in most countries remains rather hazy. There do, however, seem to have been a number of trends over the past few years, which are worthy of note:

- Corporate responsibility is becoming more of a legal issue, with statutes being passed that put more responsibility on the corporation and its officers. A good example of this are the laws relating to the duty of directors. Increasingly, the view is being taken that directors who act in an irresponsible manner should not be allowed to start up another company straight away. In the past, in many countries it was very common for unscrupulous directors to set up companies with the only aim of making these companies go bust – having purchased large amounts of goods in the meantime, of course. Such activities are no longer as easy to get away with.
- More positive acceptance of the company as a legal entity in cases of serious criminal conduct, as well as minor infringements of regulatory law. We saw the case of the Ford Pinto where a company was actually sued as an organization rather than just the individuals involved being sued. Can we ever just blame the individuals in corporate irresponsibility cases?
- Making it much clearer what the responsibilities of directors are so that it is less possible for them to 'walk away' from problems that they have caused.
- Better facilities for investigating corporate crimes.
- A more effective range of sentences that take into account a company's financial status and also minimize the adverse effects on innocent parties.

We have mentioned the *Herald of Free Enterprise* disaster on several occasions and will now consider it as a case study, as it raises a number of important questions. The primary one is this: When a small number of individuals apparently cause a disaster, can all of the blame be put on them? Is it not the responsibility of the directors of the company to devise a system that reduces the chances of disasters happening in the first place? Read the case and consider these issues.

Two Case Studies

CASE STUDY – The 'Herald of Free Enterprise'

On 6 March 1987, the British vessel *Herald of Free Enterprise* of the Townsend Thoresen Ferry fleet sank outside the Belgian port of Zeebrugge with the loss of 188 lives. Only luck prevented the loss of all 539 passengers on board. The ship had sailed out of the harbour with its bow doors open. This had made the ship capsize and turn over. It would have turned right over, but it was passing a sandbank at the time and came to rest on that. Had that not happened, the human cost would have been far greater.

At first sight, the disaster was caused by neglect by three employees on the ship. The primary cause seemed to be the assistant bosun, who was supposed to shut the doors but overslept. Another apparently guilty party was the first officer, who had been supervising the loading of vehicles but left to go to the bridge to fulfil other duties before the bosun arrived. Finally, the captain, who had overall responsibility for ensuring the ship set sail in a safe condition, did not check to see that the doors had been closed. He merely assumed that since he had heard nothing from the bosun or the first officer, that the ship was indeed seaworthy.

A formal court investigation was held. During the course of it a number of factors came to light. When the *Herald* left Zeebrugge on that fateful night, not all the water had been pumped out of the bow ballast tanks, and as such, the ship was riding some three foot lower in the water than usual at the bow. The *Herald* backed out of the berth stern first. By the time she had swung around, the bow was in darkness and the open bow doors were not obvious to the ship's captain. As the ship increased speed, a bow wave began to build under the prow. At 15 knots, with the bow down 2–3 feet lower than normal, water began to break through the open doors over the main car deck at a rate of 200 tons per minute.

In common with other 'ro-ro' (roll on, roll off) vessels, the *Herald's* main vehicle deck had no subdividing bulkheads. Conventional ships have bulkheads that split the ship up into watertight sections. Flooded sections can then be shut off should the ship begin to take on water. In the case of a ro-ro ferry, if water entered the deck it could flow from end to end or from side to side with ease. Of course, it would not be possible in a ferry to put bulkheads in because it would make the easy loading and unloading of cars impractical. In the case of the *Herald*, the flows of water through the bow doors quickly caused the vessel to become unstable. The ship listed 30 degrees to port almost instantaneously. Vast quantities continued to pour in and fill the port wing of the vehicle deck, eventually causing a capsize to port on to the sandbank.

Following the capsize, a search and rescue operation was mounted. At least 150 passengers and 38 crew members lost their lives. As with most cases like this, most people died because of exposure to the freezing water. In addition, many others were injured. Many more deaths would have occurred had it not been for the notable bravery of a number of passengers who helped many to safety, often risking their lives to do so. The death toll was the worst for a British vessel in peacetime since the *Titanic* in 1912.

The Result of the Investigation

The investigation's report named the three shipboard employees as contributing to the disaster. While it blamed the company in general, it did not single out any other individuals within the company as having actually contributed to the disaster. The tribunal concluded by rendering a verdict of unlawful killing, which implied that a crime had been committed.

Facts at the investigation made it clear that the cause of the disaster went *far beyond* the neglect of the three employees on that evening. There were a number of contributory factors, all of which had previously been known to the management and directors of the company, or had been brought to their attention by front-line operating managers.

In particular, the report identified a number of background factors, which may also have contributed to the disaster:

1. The officers were required to work 12 hours on and not less than 24 hours off duty. In contrast, each crew was on board ship for 24 hours and then had 48 hours ashore. Because of this rotation, three crews intersected five sets of officers, thus frustrating stable working relationships.
2. The Zeebrugge route was the longest ferry route in the company. As such, the company took the opportunity to reduce the number of officers from four to three on this route because the longer sailing time gave the officers not on that route more time to relax.
3. This elimination of one officer resulted in the fact that the loading officer was required to be on the car deck supervising door closure at the same time as he was required to be on the bridge overseeing the ship's departure from the dock. Written complaints about this conflict had been sent to senior management.

4. There was a commercial pressure to sail early. 'Sailing late out of Zeebrugge isn't on,' said a company memo.
5. The captain assumed the doors were closed because he did not receive a report saying that they were open. This negative system of reporting (as opposed to a positive system that would have required confirmation of closure before assuming the doors were closed) was the normal, approved operating procedure for the company.
6. There were five prior instances of ships sailing with the doors open. No incidents resulted from these prior cases of negligence. Management, who had not drawn them to the attention of the other masters, knew about some of these incidents.
7. According to the report of the investigative tribunal, the board of directors did not appreciate their responsibility for the safe management of the ships. From top to bottom, the whole organization was 'sloppy'.
8. There were no job descriptions because a senior manager felt that it was better that people defined their own roles.
9. When asked 'Who was responsible for safety?', a director replied, 'Well, in truth, nobody, though there ought to have been.' A final report said that the board of directors must accept a heavy responsibility for their 'lamentable lack of directions'.
10. Passenger overloading was a concern. One master wrote that 'This total [number of persons] is way over the life-saving capacity of the vessel. The fine for this offence is £50,000, and probably loss of certificate. May I please know what steps the company intend to take to protect my career from mistakes of this nature?'. He never received a reply.
11. Lack of door warning lights. One master had asked before if warning lights could be installed on the bridge to show that the doors were closed. Management's written reply to that request was: 'I cannot see the purpose or need for the stern door to be monitored on the bridge, as the seaman in charge of closing the doors is standing by the control panel and watching them close.'

The Zeebrugge tragedy took place against a threatening industry background. The cross-channel passenger market had reached maturity, although some growth in freight traffic was expected. The industry was consolidating in this mature market, and cuts in unit costs were vigorously pursued in several ways, such as the reduction of crew levels, the deployment of larger vessels and by speeding up of vessel turn-around times at port. The Channel Tunnel posed another major threat to the ferry industry and provided a strong impetus in the process of cost reduction.

Pause for thought ...

1. Who was responsible for the disaster?
2. What is the correct punishment here?

We can say first of all, that the assistant bosun should not have fallen asleep on duty. This is a disciplinary issue. We can also say that the other two officers had inherent responsibility because of their position. The captain, in particular, was in overall command of the ship and therefore should be responsible for its safety. There was a time when it was expected that the captain went down with his ship!

The company did not set up strong systems to prevent disasters happening. In simple terms, the fact that an individual fell asleep should not have sunk a large ship. Some of the facts are especially worrying. The fact that there were no job descriptions is really quite amazing. Even the most basic management text will tell us that safety-orientated jobs like this require highly structured, formalized work with lots of rules. Inevitably, if you have no job descriptions then there will be tasks that are duplicated and jobs that are missed. In a very creative environment, such as in an advertising agency, this might be acceptable. But not on a ship.

The negative reporting structure might also work well in a very relaxed creative environment, but again in a safety-driven one it would seem to be irresponsible. The assumption should be that there might be a problem and then to seek confirmation that all is well. The lack of provision of warning lights on the bridge is another example of this.

Clearly there was a major system problem in this case and it is a good lesson in how a poor system can make human error catastrophic. It would be good to report that this type of problem was no more. Sadly, that is not the case. First, we might comment on the sinking of the *Estonia*, another roll-on, roll-off ferry disaster that seemed to be caused by the very design of the ship. The Paddington Rail Disaster of 1999 caused considerable outrage and seems to have similar features to the *Herald of Free Enterprise* case.

CASE STUDY – **The Paddington Rail Disaster**

On 5 October 1999, one of the worst accidents in British railway history occurred. The morning rush-hour accident happened when a Thames turbo commuter train passed through a red light at Ladbroke Grove, two miles outside Paddington station in west London. The Thames train, driven by Michael Hodder, 31, collided almost head-on with a London-bound Great Western high-speed train. Both Mr Hodder and the Great Western driver, Brian Cooper, 52, were among those killed.

In total, more than 30 people were killed with another 400 people being injured in the accident, which led to rescuers fighting to free passengers from fire-engulfed and crash-damaged carriages. The UK's Health and Safety Executive that investigated the crash concluded that the initial cause of the accident appeared to be that the Thames train had passed a red signal – signal 109. However, it added that the reasons why the train had passed the red light were likely to be complex and that 'any action or omission on the part of the driver was only one such factor in a failure involving many contributory factors'.

Mr Hodder, who had joined Thames in February 1999, had only fully qualified as a driver thirteen days before the accident and had completed just nine shifts as the driver in charge. However, the HSE advised that this was not a relevant factor in the cause of the accident. The HSE report also said the signals on the gantry, which carried signal 109, were of an unusual design, which might be hard to read.

Discussion of the Case

The disaster happened against a background of worsening safety across the rail network in the UK. The UK rail network had been privatized in 1994 and there was evidence that some rail companies had been saving money by cutting corners. In particular, many railway workers thought that the safety of both passengers and workers had stopped being an issue of public concern and more of one related to profit. On the face of it, spending less money on safety and cutting corners on maintenance would mean bigger profits. Perhaps the most worrying fact was that the Paddington crash had been preceded by a similar accident in the late 1980s at Clapham, South London.

The inquiry into the 1988 Clapham rail disaster, in which 35 people died, had recommended the installation of Automatic Train Protection (ATP) across the rail network. The cost of installing ATP is around £1 billion. In the event, it wasn't for another ten years, after more deaths in the Southall crash, that the Labour government announced that a cut-price (and less effective) system, the Train Protection Warning System (TPWS), would be installed – by 2004.

Before the privatization of the network, the responsibility for ensuring safety on the railways rested with British Rail. It was felt that there were clear lines of responsibility. After the privatization of 1994, however, the view of many was that things were very different. From this time, Railtrack now subcontracted all the work on infrastructure and maintenance to other firms, many of which were not railway specialists. The result seemed to be confusion and a lack of clarity over who was responsible for what. It has also been alleged that the priority for repairs went to the most profitable lines, not to the lines that needed the repairs the most.

Another problem raised by the railway workers' unions is the question of terms and conditions. Before 1994, all safety-critical workers would work a maximum nine-hour day, not counting voluntary overtime. In the year 2000, drivers are on either ten- or eleven-hour days, depending on which company they work for. That means nine hours' actual driving time. On top of that, drivers get as little as nine hours' rest between shifts (and less if they work overtime). In most jobs now that is illegal – but not for transport workers. Along with the longer hours came tougher sickness rules, penalizing drivers who were ill 'too often'. Drivers were put under huge pressure to work even if they felt unwell.

Comparisons Between the Paddington and *Herald of Free Enterprise* Disasters

The comparison between these two events is clear. In both cases, there seems to have been evidence that disaster was inevitable. In both cases, there was evidence of cost cutting and a recognition by managers that more could have been done. In both cases, the blame was put squarely on the shoulders of the individual (a recent – July 2000 – ruling found that Hodder was primarily responsible for the Paddington crash). In both cases, though, there was much evidence that the disasters could have been avoided if better systems had been put in place.

Pause for thought . . .
Can a system that relies on individual action ever be acceptable in a transport system or similar case where people's lives are at risk? Is it not the responsibility of the company to ensure that individual action alone cannot cause such problems?

The next case looks at Levi Strauss and Co., a company that has had a number of business problems in recent years but has, nevertheless, been put forward as an excellent example of how a company can act responsibly and give a fair deal to all of its shareholders.

One Final Case Study

CASE STUDY – **Levi Strauss and Co.**

Levi Strauss and Co. has emerged as one of the world's largest clothing companies, with sales of over $1 billion. It has certainly had its financial problems of late, although these seem to be reducing. The company has won a variety of awards, including the accolade of being the most ethical private company in the USA.

Levi's ethics are not 'added on' once the main aim of making money is achieved: they are at the core of the business. The business essentially adopts an ethical strategy. Levi Strauss has had a long history of corporate responsibility. We have already noted that very often the motivation for an ethical strategy comes out of the ideals of the founder and this was certainly the case with Levi's. The company's founder, Levi Strauss, spent a lot of his time on charitable causes and the company became well known for its policy of avoiding laying off people in the recession in the 1930s. Equally notably, they ensured equal employment opportunities for African Americans in their factory during the 1950s and 1960s when they expanded into the southern states. This was very much at odds with the policies of many other companies at this time.

The company has always encouraged its employees to get involved with the local community and in 1968 a major decision was taken to enhance this by the starting up of Community Involvement Teams. There are now more than 100 of these world-wide that work towards the enhancement of the local community.

The company's efforts have included helping the poor get themselves back into work and helping people with AIDS. We have already spoken a great deal about AIDS in the workplace and the policy of Levi Straus in this regard is noteworthy. The company claims to have taken a leadership role in this area and certainly this seems to be borne out by results. In 1997, the company received the first National Business and Labour Award for Leadership on HIV/AIDS from the United States Center for Disease Control.

Levi's has expanded internationally and now more than 40 per cent of its revenues come from international business and all of their international subsidiaries work on the same basis as head office. There is no question of applying local values where it proves expedient. A key aspect of this is the Global Sourcing and Operating Guidelines produced by the company. Introduced in 1992, the aim of these is to define what the company regards as acceptable levels of practice in the workplace, including the respect of workers' rights, health and safety issues, and the environment. Suppliers that are unable or unwilling to meet these guidelines are taken off the approved supplier list.

A good example of how this is applied is in the company's sewing business. This sources product from some of the poorest countries in the world where the treatment of labour can be very poor, relative to Western values. Levi's response was to produce a policy statement on Business Partner Terms of Engagement. This sets out to its suppliers what it expects, including environmental requirements, ethical standards, health and safety, legal requirements and employment practices. An example of this was when Levi stated that they would not source goods from China. Levi's judged that many local employment practices, including the use of prison labour, breached the supplier code of practice.

The Levi's code of ethics is of interest. The primary strategy commitment is to commercial success in terms 'broader than merely financial measures'. It is worth considering what this means. Essentially, the company takes the view that success is not just about profits. This goes very much against the view of Friedman and others who would argue that profits are the only reason why a company should be in business. Levi's would argue that making the world a better place is also an important aim, which might include improving workers' conditions or showing understanding to those with disabilities, as we have seen.

Another aspect of the company's strategy, which fits in well with some of the views that we have been considering in this book, is *respect for all stakeholders*. Levi's take a stakeholder view of corporate responsibility.

This responsibility should therefore include respect for our employees' suppliers, customers, consumers and other interested parties. Above all, respect should not just be about the shareholders.

A further aspect of the Levi's code again fits in well with much of what we have been talking about in this book. This is a commitment to conduct, which is not only legal but also 'fair and morally correct in a fundamental sense'. This relates to the 'law and morality' argument that we have been following throughout the book. The 'if it's legal, it's OK' discussion has been mentioned many times. As we have said, it can be argued that providing a company follows the law of the country that it is in, then it can be said to be acting responsibly. This author, and the Levi Strauss Company, would be at odds with this view. As we have seen, the idea that if something is legal then it is OK falls down on a number of counts. First, there is the issue of morality being wider and generally ahead of legality. Laws tend to follow morals and also tend to be much more focused and less all encompassing. Another problem with this argument is that laws in different countries tend to vary a great deal. If something that is illegal in one country is illegal in ours, does that mean that we do the act in this one country and don't do it in ours? What suddenly makes it moral in one place and immoral in another? Surely there are some universally correct moral standards that should apply everywhere.

Levi's approach assumes that there are certain standards that should apply everywhere, irrespective of local customs and conditions. To a large degree this fits in with the 'universal rule' argument put forward by Kant and other deontologists. We may pay people less in a developing county but that does not give us the right to give poor working conditions or poor medical care. A human right, to be a human right, has to be universal.

Another cornerstone of Levi's ethical strategy is in the area of conflict of interest. The company aims to achieve avoidance of not only real but also the appearance of conflict of interest. In other words, low-cost production may increase profits, but there will be limits and some forms of labour may well go against the fundamental strategy adopted. There may be a conflict of interest.

Levi's also have a statement of ethical principles. This includes a commitment to seek to be honest and fair, to show respect for others and to keep promises in working relationships. Added to this is the company's Aspiration Statement. This recognizes that people need recognition for their work and positive behaviour, and makes good use of human diversity.

Another area of note is that Levi's has integrated ethics into the normal structure of management. For example, managers are not judged on performance by economic performance alone. Up to 40 per cent of management bonuses are decided on performance factors related to ethics, values and personal style as set in the Aspiration Statement and others. To help this they are given training and other methods of support including a core-training period of four days' training on ethics.

As well as the work of individual people, there is also a back-up in the form of a Social Responsibility and Ethics Committee. This is made up of senior management and has a small in-house research capability to investigate ethical issues and propose changes.

This has been a major area of Levi's since their inception. Every Levi site has a community involvement programme. The companies spend on average $16 million a year on such activities. It also encourages their workers to get involved with charities. Finally, Levi's was one of the first companies to use disabled people in advertising and has generally adopted a human-rights view of promotion.

Corporate Responsibility

The notion of a company being responsible for its actions from an ethical point of view is a relatively new one, but one that is certainly gaining ground. Having said that, as we have seen with the recent Paddington disaster in the UK, there is still a tendency to blame the individual and ignore the 'big picture'. Whilst individuals should be punished for major mistakes, it is arguably naïve and irresponsible not to set up systems that minimize the charges of human error. Organizations can and should act in a more responsible way and many are indeed doing so. The case of Levi Strauss is not unique.

The Future of Business Ethics

This book has discussed a number of fundamental questions in business. The subject of business ethics, I believe, will become increasingly important as time goes on. What will the future hold? There are a variety of views on this. The consensus seems to be that the future will be one of more and more group and project working – although often, the people involved may not even be in the same room or even on the same continent. The steady implementation of faster and more powerful technology will mean less time spent on routine tasks. If we accept this prediction, then the world is likely to become more open. The 'cover ups' of the past are less likely to occur. On the other hand, all of that technology is going to present even more opportunities to act unethically if we so wish. Of course, the very concept of what is right and wrong may change. Business ethics is a very fluid subject. It may have its roots in the past, but it looks very firmly to the future.

Bibliography and Recommended Reading

The subject of business ethics is very dynamic and for this reason, students of the subject are recommended to read major business magazines on a regular basis. A very strong source of further material is the Internet. Below are references for the materials referred to in the text along with further information about texts and Internet URLs for further study:

References and Recommended Further Reading

Chryssides, G. and Kaler, J. *An Introduction to Business Ethics*. London, Chapman and Hall, 1995.

Green, R. M. *The Ethical Manager: A New Method for Business Ethics*. New York, Macmillan, 1994.

Kant, I. *Grundlegung zur Metaphysik der Sitten* (trans. K. Volnader). Hamburg, F. Meiner Verlag, 1965/1785.

Locke, J. *Second Treatise on Civil Government*, J. W. Gough (ed.). Oxford, Oxford University Press.

Velasquez, M. *Business Ethics, Concepts and Cases*. Englewood Cliffs, NJ, Prentice Hall, 1992.

Watts, M., 'Black Gold, White Heat', in S. Pile and K. Michael (eds), *Geographies of Resistance*, London, Routledge.

Useful web sites

www.lawnewsnetwork.com/practice/employmentlaw/news
www.wa.gov/dop/helpacademy/resource/Crsxharr.htm
caselaw.findlaw.com

www.equalrights.org
www.hrlawindex.com
www.employerspublications.com/harass_explain.html
www.globalpolicy.org/socecon/tcns/humrig.htm
ethics.acusd.edu/index.html
commfaculty.fullertonb.edu/lester/ethics/ethics
www.essentialaction.org/shell/issues.html
www.oneworld.org/mosop
www.economist.com/archive/view.eg
www.news.bbc.co.uk
www.oneworld.org/pwbf
www.sustainability.co.uk/about-SA/shell-relationship.htm

Index